Intelligent Disobedience

Doing Right When What You're Told to Do Is Wrong

Intelligent Disobedience

Doing Right When What You're Told to Do Is Wrong

Ira Chaleff

BK°

Berrett–Koehler Publishers, Inc.
a BK Life book

Berrett-Koehler Publishers, Inc.
1333 Broadway, Suite 1000
Oakland, CA 94612-1921
Tel: (510) 817-2277   Fax: (510) 817-2278   www.bkconnection.com

Ordering Information

Quantity sales. Special discounts are available on quantity purchases by corporations, associations, and others. For details, contact the "Special Sales Department" at the Berrett-Koehler address above.

Individual sales. Berrett-Koehler publications are available through most bookstores. They can also be ordered directly from Berrett-Koehler: Tel: (800) 929-2929; Fax: (802) 864-7626; www.bkconnection.com

Orders for college textbook/course adoption use. Please contact Berrett-Koehler: Tel: (800) 929-2929; Fax: (802) 864-7626.

Orders by U.S. trade bookstores and wholesalers. Please contact Ingram Publisher Services, Tel: (800) 509-4887; Fax: (800) 838-1149; E-mail: customer.service@ingrampublisherservices.com; or visit www.ingrampublisherservices.com/Ordering for details about electronic ordering.

Berrett-Koehler and the BK logo are registered trademarks of Berrett-Koehler Publishers, Inc.

Printed in Canada

Berrett-Koehler books are printed on long-lasting acid-free paper. When it is available, we choose paper that has been manufactured by environmentally responsible processes. These may include using trees grown in sustainable forests, incorporating recycled paper, minimizing chlorine in bleaching, or recycling the energy produced at the paper mill.

Library of Congress Cataloging-in-Publication Data

Chaleff, Ira.
Intelligent disobedience : doing right when what you're told to do is wrong / Ira Chaleff. -- First edition.
     pages cm
  ISBN 978-1-62656-427-5 (pbk.)
  1. Right and wrong. 2. Authority. 3. Obedience. 4. Decision making--Moral and ethical aspects. I. Title.
  BJ1411.C43 2015
  170'.44--dc23
                                                    2015008298

First Edition
20 19 18 17 16 15   10 9 8 7 6 5 4 3 2 1

Interior design and project management: Dovetail Publishing Services
Cover design: Brad Foltz

To the young and the not so young
who make decisions to obey or not to obey,
conscious of their personal responsibility for the outcome
regardless of which decision they make,
no matter who gave the order.

Contents

How I Learned About Intelligent Disobedience

Wᴀʏ ᴇxᴀᴄᴛʟʏ ɪs Iɴᴛᴇʟʟɪɢᴇɴᴛ Dɪsᴏʙᴇᴅɪᴇɴᴄᴇ? I had the same question when I first heard the term. These are two words that don't usually fit together.

We know what obedience is: following orders or rules or established ways of doing things. Obeying usually keeps life running smoothly. Disobedience is a contrary response to these common obligations of life. Disobeying often results in unpleasant consequences. Those issuing the orders or setting the rules are inclined to enforce them, and they usually have the power to do so. Therefore, it's reasonable to ask, under what circumstances can disobedience be considered intelligent?

I suspect you would agree that those with the authority to issue orders or to establish rules are not infallible. You've experienced that reality, perhaps more often than you'd like. In some circumstances, the information on which authorities are basing a specific order or rule may be incomplete, old, or plain wrong. Their intentions may be excellent, but their assessment of the situation and their judgment may be faulty. Or the order may be ethically problematic. In these circumstances, implementing that order or rule would probably lead to an undesirable outcome, perhaps even a dangerous one. It would be better to question the order rather than obey it. That would be Intelligent Disobedience.

This seems like common sense, yet it can be a difficult thing to do. People like to believe they would have the courage to resist an order that would cause harm. Contrary to this belief, research and history show us that in many situations the majority will obey. Depending on the circumstances, perhaps you would obey.

The purpose of this book is to help individuals at all stages of human development, and in all types of work, achieve the awareness and skills to avoid the "just following orders" trap. Regardless of the pressure we feel to obey those in authority, we are accountable for our actions. We need to be able to take a stand and do the right thing when what we are told to do is wrong. If we do this well, even those issuing the wrong orders will benefit from our having made the right choice.

I first heard the term *Intelligent Disobedience* when I was teaching a class on leader-follower relationships to a group of mid-level managers. We were at the point in the class where I introduce the question "When is it appropriate to obey authority and when should authority be questioned?" This is a central question for all of us who live in complex societies and who work or study in hierarchies in which other people have the authority to give us directions.

A woman seated to my left raised her hand and said,

"I have an example of this under the table."

The whole class joined me in a moment of collectively being startled by her statement. What did she mean, "under the table"?

Her classmates had stopped paying attention to the unusual act of bringing a dog to class every morning. She was low key about it and the dog rested quietly, almost invisibly, at her feet. I taught only one day of the students' two-week course. In my focus on making sure the room and equipment were properly set up, I had failed to register this student was accompanied by a dog. So much for my powers of observation!

She went on to explain,

"I am helping to train a guide dog that will assist an individual who is blind. At my stage of training, the dog is learning to be comfortable in busy social situations and to obey all the basic

commands she will be given when working as a guide dog. When I finish this part of her program, she will go to a more skilled trainer who will teach her Intelligent Disobedience."

My ears perked up more or less like a dog that has just heard something that grabs its attention!

"What do you mean by Intelligent Disobedience?" I asked, intuitively attracted to this term I had never heard before.

"Most of the time," she continued, *"it's really important that the dog obeys the human's instructions. But sometimes it would be dangerous to do so; for example, when a man with limited sight gave the command to step off a curb just as a quiet hybrid car was turning into the street. The dog must know not to obey a command that will put the team—human and dog—in danger. Learning not to obey is a higher order of skill. It will require a trainer who is more experienced than I am."*

Here was an example right under my nose of what I had been thinking and writing about for fifteen years! It is part of the socialization process in any human culture to teach our young to obey. Some cultures do it in harsh, authoritarian ways, and others do so more gently. However it is accomplished, children must be responsive to formal authority as they grow into adulthood. As adults, they must be responsive to the formal authorities in their organizations' chains of command.

If the kindergarten teacher asks everyone to rest quietly for fifteen minutes, the students must do so and not pester the kids next to them whose eyes are closed. If the football coach says no partying the night before the game, a player must resist temptation from peer pressure to party or face being sidelined. The examples are endless of how we teach and reinforce the obedience that the culture requires.

But how do we teach obedience without teaching it *too well*? This isn't a question that is sufficiently considered. There are enough examples of young people acting out in *defiance* of authority that, understandably, the attention goes to correcting or penalizing this deviance. Though the defiant might create social nuisances at times, they are not necessarily a danger. They may even prove to be productively rebellious innovators!

The danger lies in teaching obedience too well, so the habit of unquestioning obedience is carried into adulthood. We see the results of this when employees in corporations, government agencies, the military, and elsewhere bow to pressure to do things that cover up problems and create unnecessary risk or damage. Even more disturbing are the number of historic events in which crimes against humanity have been committed because people were "just following orders."

This book will examine how the skills of Intelligent Disobedience can be taught and exercised in a variety of settings and why they are, literally, a matter of life and death in many of those settings. It will show why the smart parent, teacher, or organization leader will value Intelligent Disobedience and how they can foster it. Whatever your own role, it will help you develop the skills and strategies to do right even when under social pressure to do something you believe is wrong.

A guide dog that is entrusted with the safety of a human being cannot afford to make a serious error even once. Without knowing when and how to disobey, guide dogs would lose their value of keeping the team safe. We have something important to learn from the training given to these best of man's best friends and how to adapt it to human development.

Foreword

FRENCH PHILOSOPHER PAUL RICOEUR introduced the concept of the "servile will" in *The Symbolism of Evil*, (1960).[1] The servile will is the will that makes itself a slave to authority. It diminishes human nature. Such a mental state, although seemingly extreme, is more commonplace than we would like to believe. There is a sense of freedom in liberating oneself from a will that is enslaved.

From our earliest socialization, we are rewarded for obeying all authorities: parents, teachers, religious leaders, politicians, and more. Nowhere in our educational system, or even our social system of values, is there training in appropriate disobedience or simply to distinguish between obedience to just authority and defying unjust authority.

In our private and public institutions, we see perennial catastrophic results of this failure among adults who should know better, but conform, comply, and obey anyone who conveys a sense of authority. In the schooling of our young, we see patterns of obedience being formed that lead to misplaced obedience when they become the adults in those institutions. Where do we turn to for fresh answers to striking the right balance between obedience to authority and independent choice?

We can turn to two places. First we turn to traditional social sciences for research-based answers and maybe solutions. Then we turn in a totally new direction, to be revealed to you in this remarkable book, about what we can learn from the training of trusted guide dogs who are taught what is called Intelligent Disobedience.

It is has been a half century since the great social science experiments on authority and obedience, first by Stanley Milgram at Yale

University in the 1960s, then followed by my Stanford Prison Experiment in the early 1970s. Milgram's work revealed that among ordinary citizens, two-thirds were willing to deliver painful shocks at the insistence of an authority who was a stranger to them. The good news in that research program was that when participants observed people like themselves refusing to deliver the painful shocks, then 90 percent of them refused. That means we are prone to obey authority, but also affected by the behavior of our peers. Thus we are all social role models, and what we do—for good or for bad—has a ripple effect when other people observe us.

My research at Stanford University extended the Milgram paradigm away from a single authority issuing commands to having participants embedded in a social context where the power resided in the situation. Normal, healthy college students, randomly assigned roles of prisoner or guard, lived in a simulated prison setting—prisoners did so day and night, the guards for eight-hour shifts. We intended the study to run for two weeks but had to terminate it after six days because it had run out of control.

Our goal was to create the mindset in these college student participants that they were real prisoners and real guards in a real prison. That goal was accomplished far beyond what I could imagine when we began. In the contest between good people and evil situation, humanity lost and the situation won. Put differently, the dispositions of the individuals predicted nothing about how they behaved in either condition when overwhelmed by a powerful, novel social setting.

Even I was caught up in the power of that situation by mistakenly playing dual roles of principal investigator and prison superintendent. In the latter role, I became indifferent to the suffering of these young men, allowing the guard abuse that emerged to continue much longer than it should have. The takeaway message from this study is that human behavior is more under the control of situational influences than we want to believe, as we continue to cherish the concept of freedom of the will and inner determination of our behavior.

More recently, I have been conducting research in the Netherlands and Sicily, with my colleague Piero Bocchiaro, to illuminate the conditions that can lead to disobedience to unjust authority. We introduce the concept of productive disobedience, an act of peaceful noncompliance with laws or norms or the demands of authority that, if followed, would hinder the moral progress of society.

What happens when a scenario is described to college students that clearly depicts an authority figure making unethical and unjust demands on student participants, and they describe how they would react? The vast majority report they would rebel; however, when their classmates are actually put into that very same situation, just the opposite occurs—more than 80 percent blindly obey! This again reveals the power of situational norms to dominate moral reasoning.

Our only bright light was discovering that those high on the anti-authoritarian personality trait were best able to be defiant. We found disobedience could be enhanced when in the presence of student rebels and when obedience had a high personal cost. The overall high rate of obedience to authority was, however, distressingly high.

Despite my proselytizing these messages for many years, humanity is no closer to having absorbed the lessons of these experiments than it was before they were made part of our social consciousness. In our private and public institutions, we still see perennial catastrophic results of this failure among adults who should know better. It is evident in the schooling of our young where we see patterns of rigid obedience being formed from day one by teachers and officials. This leads, in turn, to misplaced obedience when these students become the adults and taxpayers supporting those institutions. Nowhere is there any attempt to teach the fundamental difference between just and unjust authority, the former earning our respect, the latter justifying disobedience and rebellion.

Where do we turn for fresh answers for striking the right balance between rigid, mindless obedience to authority and independent choice? Our society gives lip service to creating independent thinkers as a primary result of all education. But so far, there is not much to show for the success of that ideal.

I was surprised to discover the answers I was seeking in this remarkable book by Ira Chaleff. He offers us a metaphor and an effective model from "man's best friend." It is clear that we painstakingly teach guide dogs how to discern between when to obey and when to resist in order to avoid causing harm if given dangerous commands. Surely, we can do the same in the acculturation of our young and the development of our professionals in the highly sensitive roles that our society gives them to make things run properly. Whether training teachers for classroom management, guards for the security roles that have become ubiquitous, or information specialists who control our privacy and the protection of our identity, it is crucial to develop new ways of distinguishing between appropriate obedience and rightful disobedience.

Reading this remarkable book has given me new hope for the prospect of humanity finally learning the overdue lessons needed to cope effectively with the many urgent challenges of our times. I do hope that you, dear reader, will also learn and apply the vital messages contained in Intelligent Disobedience. It is our communal responsibility to see that its lessons will be taught in relevant ways at every stage of human and professional development—to our youth, as well as to our social, religious, business, and political leaders.

Philip Zimbardo
Creator of the Stanford Prison Experiment, 2014

Creating Cultures that Do the Right Thing

INTELLIGENT DISOBEDIENCE IS ABOUT finding the healthy balance for living in a system with rules and authorities while maintaining our own responsibility for the actions we take.

In recent years, a school of thought emerged regarding different types of intelligence. Knowing when and how to obey or disobey authority can be considered a form of intelligence that incorporates both interpersonal skills and moral grounding.

Obedience is often a reflex, not a rational decision. There is a primal instinct to obey authority, reinforced by a steep price for violating social norms. Reflexive rather than thinking obedience sooner or later leads to poor or damaging outcomes.

The project of this book is to examine how to change that reflexive habit into a conscious choice of whether to obey or to dissent in a specific situation. On a larger scale, its aspiration is to encourage the culture to embrace Intelligent Disobedience as a valued aspect of one's identity and an antidote to authoritarianism.

Nearly daily, we find stories in the media of individuals and whole departments who went along with programs or orders that came from higher levels in- or outside their organization that defy common sense, our values as a people, or the law of the land.

No segment of our culture is immune, from politics to sports, from federal agencies to religious institutions, from the education system to law enforcement, from health care to transportation, from food production and distribution to communications, from the military to financial services, from energy to social services.

You've read these stories or seen them in the media and, like me, wondered, *How could they have done that?* The question now is *How do we change this?*

Change will be achieved by teaching and rewarding the skills to differentiate between programs or orders that should be embraced and those that should be questioned, examined, and at times resisted. The capacity to do this should be an integral part of risk management strategies, which exist in all sectors.

If we distill Intelligent Disobedience down to a formula, it would look something like this:

1. Understand the mission of the organization or group, the goals of the activity of which you are a part, and the values that guide how to achieve those goals.

2. When you receive an order that does not seem appropriate to the mission, goals, and values, clarify the order as needed, then pause to further examine the problem with it, whether that involves its safety, effectiveness, cultural sensitivity, legality, morality, or common decency.

3. Make a conscious choice whether to comply with the order or to resist it and offer an acceptable alternative when there is one.

4. Assume personal accountability for your choice, recognizing that if you obey the order, you are still accountable regardless of who issued the order.

Formulas give us a sense of where we are going but are not sufficient to transform deeply seated cultural patterns. Transformation requires first understanding the powerful social mechanisms that produce and reward obedience, regardless of the merit or lack of merit in what is being obeyed. Then strategies and tools for overriding these mechanisms and retaining independence of thought and action are needed.

I did not start writing this book because I had the answers for how to do this. I began writing because I wanted to learn more about the answers. That requires a journey. When an author embarks on such a journey, in a sense the author is in service to the book. As the book unfolds, it insists the author look more deeply into the matters under investigation.

The author can report a symptom, but the book demands to know what is the underlying disease? The author can identify the disease and the book insists on knowing what caused it? What are its triggers? The author digs deeper and identifies causes for the disease and the book says, now what? Are there cures for this disease? If so, please share them with the reader. If not, how can we manage the disease until a cure is found? What are lines of investigation the reader and other researchers can follow to develop better ways of managing and ultimately curing the disease?

This book has taken me on such a journey. Professionally, I work as a consultant and a coach to adults who make our government agencies, armed services, corporations, professional service firms, nonprofit associations, and universities run. I have seen these organizations from the bottom and from the top. I know the pressures that exist at different levels and the difficult choices that have to be made about what is the right thing to do in different situations.

I could have written this book to solely address these professional environments. The reader would have recognized the book as a work about organizational behavior and ethical and operational choices. But if I left the book at that level, we would have been examining the symptoms or, at best, the disease. We would not have explored the causes of the condition and the remedies for those causes.

Let me put it this way: no executive, manager, front-line worker, administrator, principal or teacher, officer or foot soldier sprang fully formed from Zeus's head. They—you—were raised in a family that was embedded in a culture, and each family, culture, and subculture within that culture developed ways of socializing its young, including you.

In contemporary society, socialization occurs most intensively in a formal school setting. If we include preschool and kindergarten, most of us spend nearly two hundred days a year for at least fourteen years in a system that is not only expected to educate us, but requires us to recognize and obey the authorities and rules of the system. When behavior shows up in our adult life at work, in the military, in our citizenship, it has been shaped to some degree by social forces that run deep. This book is going to take you diving below the surface of your working world into these formative conditions. Why?

There are at least three compelling reasons for you to accompany me on this journey. First, it is the intention of this book to help you as an individual alter some of the conditioning that is not serving you or your workplace well; it is difficult to do this without understanding the nature of the forces that are holding existing behaviors of obedience in place.

Second, if you are an executive, manager, supervisor, officer, minister, teacher, or anyone with others in your care, and you want to create an environment in which individuals hold themselves personally accountable for doing the right thing, you need to understand the underlying, shaping forces working against this in order to transform those forces.

Third, you are not only your professional role. You are a whole person. I am writing to the whole person. You may have, or expect to have children, or you may be an aunt or uncle, a mentor, a coach, or otherwise a steward of the next generation. How are those children being raised? Will the meta-messages they are getting in the current system equip them to be strong adults who can take difficult stands and to be strong citizens who can protect the values of our culture? You cannot "outsource" their moral development to the formal education process or even to the religious education process. You are part of their moral development, and you are their advocate in the system to which you entrust their development.

I am asking you to join me in an inquiry. We will:

- Look at the cultural forces that implicitly and explicitly value obedience over the higher level skill of discerning when it is and is not right to obey

- Glean scarce but useful lessons from education and training that support knowing when and how to intelligently disobey

- Examine critical research on reducing the pressure for individuals to conform and obey when they should not

- Look at cautionary examples of individuals who obeyed when they should not have and the price they paid for doing so

- Learn from uplifting examples of individuals who did the right thing when told to do the wrong thing

- Meet wise and accomplished leaders who have developed the capacity to do the right thing in those whom they serve

- Consider how the attributes of Intelligent Disobedience are central to a culture that values accountability, human dignity, and creative innovation

This book will flow among different levels of our lives—our work lives, our education lives, our home lives, back to our work lives. Understanding appropriate obedience and Intelligent Disobedience at each level will reinforce our capacity to create the right balance between these at the other levels. Throughout the journey, the image of the guide dog will accompany us, utterly devoted to obeying when doing so serves the common good and to disobeying when doing so prevents avoidable harm. We will look closely at the "secret sauce" that goes into guide dog training and distill what of this can be transferred to human development and cultural change.

There is one cautionary note I must make, though I find doing so painful. In the United States, and undoubtedly in other countries, the dominant culture is given more leeway to disobey than are others. As we have seen far too often in the United States, when people of color, and especially young men of color, even hesitate momentarily to obey, they can pay a very steep price at the hands of those with authority, especially when that authority is armed. I caution anyone reading this book to be mindful of unwritten cultural norms and factor those into your decisions on when to obey and when and how to intelligently disobey.

Although this book explores the social roots of obedience, it is primarily a book intended for application. I am not generally a fan of distilling complex dynamics to actionable bullet points. I have nevertheless done so at the end of each chapter to aid application. In many of the chapters, the research and lessons examined contain too many riches to easily retain in one reading. Rather than risk letting them be lost, I chose to risk oversimplifying them. The task falls to you to integrate these summaries meaningfully into your thinking and actions.

You now have a map for the journey you will be taking from the workplace to the school room to the dinner table, back to the workplace, and ultimately to the responsibilities of a free citizenry. Let's start the inquiry by looking at a concrete example. It is critical to take this material out of the theoretical and the ideal into the hard realities of the world in which they play out—in other words into your world.

CHAPTER ONE

The Pressure to Obey:
What Would You Do?

I WAS TEACHING A CLASS on courageous followership to a group of doctoral candidates at a Methodist university. Courageous followership is a way of being in relation to leaders. It requires giving those in leadership roles genuine support and building relationships with them that will allow those in follower roles to speak candidly when needed to prevent or correct leadership failures. It was a great class with lots of lively, engaged dialogue. During a break, one of the students came up to me and told a story that made a deep impression on me. This story happened twenty years prior to our conversation.

She had been a young nurse, fresh out of nursing school and assigned to a hospital emergency room. A cardiac patient was rushed in. After a quick assessment, the emergency room physician ordered her to administer the medication he judged the patient needed. She was stunned because she had been taught that this particular medication carried grave risks for a cardiac patient.

For a moment, put yourself in her shoes—in those days, probably uniform white shoes. This was an era when nearly all physicians were male, all nurses female, so the gender-based inequality of power was pronounced. The physician was older and more experienced, so this added to the perceived power differential. And, after all, he was a physician, with years more training than she had! Can you feel how many social forces were at work pushing her to snap to and do what she was told? Can you sense the time pressure to act one way or another with a cardiac patient's life at stake?

She confided that she did not know where the needed courage came from to speak back to this authority figure. She told the doctor that she had been taught that particular medication could be fatal in this patient's situation.

What was the doctor's response? As is so often the case with someone in authority, he bristled at the questioning of his decision and in a raised voice, with a stern glare told her, *"You just do it!"*

Imagine yourself in that moment. You are in an emergency room. You chose nursing as a profession to help people. You want to be a competent, caring professional. If you act against your training and administer the medication and the patient dies, how are you going to feel? How will you face the patient's family? How will you face a review board that examines actions that were taken? There is no "do-over." But what if the doctor is right and you disobey? What if your refusal to act endangers the life you are trying to save? How will you live with that? And what will be the repercussions of disobedience on your career that you have just spent several years preparing for?

There's no time to hesitate. What would you do?

Seriously, what would you do?

We don't face such obvious life and death choices like this every day, but it is just such a choice that requires us to think about our accountability for obeying or disobeying, regardless of who gave the order. And it gives us a chance to mentally rehearse what it feels like to be under great pressure from an authority figure to do something we feel may be wrong, or even very wrong. When under pressure like this, our ability to make rational or moral calculations may freeze as we are flooded with stress hormones. Our ability to think outside the two choices—obey or disobey—may shut us off from productive alternative responses. The decision to question a forcefully given order usually must be made in a situation of high emotional stress.

Will that excuse the choice you make? Will that allow you to fall back on "I was just following orders"?

If you've allowed yourself to feel what this young nurse must have been feeling, you realize that you're at the point where you are going to need to take a deep breath, pump some oxygen to the brain, and quiet your fear sufficiently to make a principled decision.

So I invite you to actually do that now, to keep experiencing what she must have felt like. Take a deep breath. Take a moment. Think about alternatives to responding to the situation you suddenly find yourself in.

Now let's return to the emergency room to see what the young nurse did. This is a paraphrase of what she told me:

> *"I hooked up the IV bag to the patient, and I injected the medication the doctor had ordered into the bag. Then I called the doctor over and told him the medication was ready to be administered. All that was needed was to open the valve on the IV bag, but that I couldn't do it because it violated my training. He would need to open the valve himself."*

Do you see how she found a stance that was neither obeying nor disobeying, but stayed true to the principles she had been taught? Most of the groups to which I tell the story at this point let out low sounds of admiration for the way this newly minted professional found the composure to hold her ground. I certainly do. I am not at all sure that I would have had the presence of mind to generate the option she chose in that intense situation. That is the value of sharing stories. They mentally rehearse us for times when we find ourselves in similar, intense situations.

What was the outcome of this story?

> *The nurse's requirement that the doctor himself open the valve, if he was indeed convinced that his order was correct, stopped him in his tracks. It was enough to get him to rethink the risks and the other*

options that were available. He changed his order to administer a different medication, which the nurse promptly did. The patient recovered fully.

What was going on here? Was this an incompetent doctor? Probably not. Just as we put ourselves in the nurse's shoes, we need to put ourselves in the doctor's shoes. He may have been doing his residency at the hospital, a requirement for all physicians. Hospital residencies are infamous for the brutally long hours they require, particularly in the period this occurred. It could be that he was sleep deprived and that his own mental processes were operating at a reduced level. Emergency rooms can be particularly hectic places where the patient load suddenly spikes as several ambulances arrive at once, or violently ill patients begin retching or having seizures in the waiting area. Maybe the doctor himself had a touch of illness he was working over.

None of these conjectures are to excuse bad decisions; they are offered to humanize the authority figure. Whether a doctor, factory manager, fast-food supervisor, school principal, financial executive, or athletic coach, sometimes those in authority are not at their best, yet the responsibilities of their position require them to act. We must be able to see them as both having legitimate authority and human frailty, and at times be prepared to question them, correct them, or even disobey them. Because we can't say "we were just following orders."

Remember that nurse. There is one great role model, whatever your profession.

A few initial lessons we can glean from our engagement with this story:

1. The need for Intelligent Disobedience can arise suddenly and demand a high order of poise to respond appropriately within the compressed time the situation demands.

2. We must give our own perceptions, training, and values equal validity to the perspectives of those in authority when weighing the right course of action.

3. There are often options other than "obey" or "disobey" that can lead to better outcomes.

4. If we take a deep breath and pause to think, we may be able to offer alternative creative responses that satisfy the authority and better meet the need of the situation.

CHAPTER TWO

Obedience and Disobedience: When Is Which Right?

*"If a man can only obey and not disobey, he is a slave;
if he can only disobey and not obey, he is a rebel; he
acts out of anger, disappointment, resentment, yet
not in the name of a conviction or a principle."*

ERICH FROMM

To understand appropriate obedience and disobedience, let's reconsider the scenario in the previous chapter.

We saw the nurse resist what she thought to be a destructive order. Her skillful resistance caused the physician to reflect on his own reasoning and to take a different, presumably safer course. The patient recovered and the story had a happy ending. We know, however, that it could have played out differently.

Was it the success of the patient outcome that made this an act of Intelligent Disobedience as opposed to outright insubordination? Or were there intrinsic factors that made it Intelligent Disobedience, regardless of the outcome? To answer this we need to examine our concepts of obedience and disobedience.

Most cultures have a bias that obedience is good and disobedience is bad. If you doubt that, read the same sentence in reverse: *Most cultures have a bias that disobedience is good and obedience is bad.* That doesn't make sense to us because it isn't true. Why is that?

All human society must be organized around certain rules. How will we live together? How will we defend ourselves against hostile forces? How will we make decisions that affect the community? How will we respond to those who don't follow the rules the community has developed?

To Obey or Not to Obey

We recognize that to enjoy the many benefits of community and organization requires a degree of voluntary, and at times involuntary, obedience to the norms. This is the default position in society. It has been observed that there are three components to appropriate obedience:

1. The system we are part of is reasonably fair and functioning.

2. The authority figure setting the rule or giving the order is legitimate and reasonably competent.

3. The order itself is reasonably constructive.[1]

I am inserting the term *reasonably* into these conditions because we are dealing with imperfect human systems and human beings. In many situations, "reasonably so" is the realistic standard. In a few situations, such as the safety of nuclear power plants, the standard must be higher.

In the nurse's case, the first two conditions were present. The third was not. If all three had been present, then obedience was the appropriate default response, not because she had been given an order but because it was an order that appeared correct and did not violate her own knowledge of the situation.

The nurse didn't consciously ask herself if the system was fair; that was to her a given. Nor did she have reason to question the second component. It was presumed the doctor was a real doctor, with appropriate training and credentials. The third component, however, triggered an alarm: based on the information she had, the order, if executed, could be harmful, maybe deadly.

The Simplest Test

This is the simplest test, and often the most practical test, for Intelligent Disobedience: based on the information we have and the context in which the order is given, if obeying is likely to produce more harm than good, disobeying is the right move, at least until we have further clarified the situation and the order.

Why is that so hard to do? We are wired to obey. It is an evolutionary adaptation for allowing the growth of complex human organization and society. A general summary of works by developmental social psychologists such as Jean Piaget and Lawrence Kohlberg tell us that although our tendency to obey is strong, our reasons for obeying evolve as we grow:

> *At first we obey because our parents say to: "authority is always right."*
>
> *Then we obey because we become aware of the social rewards and penalties for obeying and disobeying: gold stars for the former, after-school detention for the latter.*
>
> *Later we obey because we realize the need for society to have the predictability that rules and laws bring: confidence that everyone at the four-way stop sign will wait their turn.*
>
> *Ultimately, if our moral development isn't stunted, we obey because we realize the intrinsic value of the rule or order in the context in which it applies.*[2]

In the nurse's situation, she in fact was obeying, but not the ill-conceived order. She was obeying a higher set of values that had grown up with her developmentally: values of placing human life and safety above her own fear of reprisal; of adhering to her hard-won training; of maintaining professionalism in a crisis situation. She discerned that the order was not correct, given the context and its potential for causing more harm than good. Whether consciously or instinctively, she chose to obey the higher level values, which directed her to take a stand.

Are there higher level values we all share as a guide for the choices we make? It does not appear life is so simple. A brief examination of history shows how dramatically values can change in a culture over the short space of a few generations. We can see the variation there is in the weight given to similar values in different cultures or even among different families. Values that we hold dearly conflict with other values we hold and may shift in importance as we change or the realities around us change.

Despite this, there are some values worth standing up for, regardless of shifting cultural mores. We may conceive of these values as inherent in life, as emanating from a higher source, as a rational way to live, or as aspirations for the people we wish to become. Regardless, there is an inner sense of values to which we can refer when faced with difficult choices. This is sometimes referred to as an inner voice. However that inner voice has come to be, if we recognize and honor that voice, it becomes the internal balance to the social pressures exerted upon us.

The Value of Obedience

Still, as we have seen, obedience is our default mode. Is this good?

Obedience is not itself good or bad. It is the context in which it occurs that gives it positive or negative value. Obedience can even be a malicious act. How? The person receiving the order knows that implementing it will have adverse consequences but implements it anyway because it will make the authority who issued the order look bad and be publicly discredited for issuing it. Leaders, beware of creating an environment in which you insist on unwavering obedience!

If obedience is not itself good or bad, neither is disobedience. Let's imagine that this particular nurse had issues with authority figures. Many people do. If she remained developmentally unaware of these issues, she might respond to the physician's order not based on reason but from an unconscious need to assert her independence.

I once sat in a dentist's chair having a cavity prepared for a filling. Each time the dentist drilled and thought the tooth had been prepared, his dental assistant would check and tell him it wasn't good enough. The first time or two this could seem like a healthy collaboration on their part. After the fifth time, it was evident there was a power struggle occurring. The result was the enamel in my tooth was drilled too thin and broke, requiring more extensive repair of the tooth.

The last thing a physician needs in an emergency room is a nurse acting out unresolved authority issues. The correct default stance in that context is prompt, accurate obedience to legitimate authority issuing appropriate professional orders.

Although we often rail against authority, there is a great benefit to systems in which it is clear who has the authority to establish rules and issue orders: it avoids endless conflict between competing ideas. There are always different goals that can be pursued and different ways of pursuing them. If each individual insists on his or her preference, or each faction on theirs, the result is paralysis, or worse, internal warfare. In healthy systems, dialogue is encouraged to inform the best possible decision. But once all voices have been heard and a decision is made by those with the authority to make it, if no core values are being violated, supporting that decision is the correct mode.

Let me underline this point by referring back to the inspiration for this story, the trusted guide dog whose core value is keeping the human in its care safe. We will examine the training that equips it to do this in a later chapter. For the moment, keep in mind that the young dog is first socialized to obey the rules and commands it needs to know. Only when the dog is socialized is it taught the equally critical skills of Intelligent Disobedience.

Deciding Whether to Obey

There are underlying rules operating in any group that enable its members to reach decisions as situations arise that require making choices. There are likely two related rule sets, or what we might call social algorithms, running at once in the guide dog or in the human being about how to respond to a command or order. The first is the algorithm of obedience:

- I am receiving a rule or order from a legitimate source, not from a random direction.

- I understand the rule or order, what its goal is and what is expected of me in achieving that goal.

- The order is good, or at least neutral in terms of the impact it will have.

- Because no serious harm will result from implementing the order and no core value is being violated, I will obey the order.

This is the dominant algorithm that we use most of the time. If we didn't, life would deteriorate into endless conflict.

The parallel and balancing algorithm is of Intelligent Disobedience. It is used far less, but when it is called for it is crucial that it override the obedience algorithm:

- The rule or order is not coming from a legitimate source or the legitimate source is missing important information that is relevant to the rule or order.

- The goal itself is wrong given the situation, or it is right but the rule or order won't achieve that goal.

- If implemented, the order will violate core values and is likely to cause serious harm.

- Instead of implementing the rule or order, I will resist it as effectively as I can, while contributing to finding a better way for moving forward.

As in guide dog development, so should it be in human development. Teach both necessary obedience and appropriate disobedience. Teach when. Teach how. Today, in nursing education programs we can be comforted knowing that nurses are given examples of situations in which they are required to query an order and, when necessary, to raise that query to a higher level. This does not mean it is necessarily easier to do so in the face of authority than it was when the nurse in our story intuitively did the right thing. But the groundwork has been laid. That is a start.

Different than Civil Disobedience

When people first hear the term *Intelligent Disobedience*, they wonder if it is the same as civil disobedience. The two are not the same.

There is, of course, a moral dimension to the assessment of whether to obey an order. Sometimes that moral dimension goes beyond questioning a specific order; it questions the legitimacy of the entire system in which the order is given. In assessing the options for correcting the system, for making it more just and inclusive, individuals or groups may conclude that the effective course is to publicly violate the systems' laws or rules. They do this in the hopes of raising others' awareness and support for change. That is civil disobedience.

The actions of civil disobedience are intentionally disruptive and often result in arrests of the violators and in media attention for the cause at hand. This is quite different from the actions of Intelligent Disobedience, which do not flagrantly violate existing laws nor usually challenge the whole system. In order to draw the distinction between Intelligent Disobedience and civil disobedience, let's do the following thought exercise.

Imagine that the emergency room scenario described in the last chapter had taken place in the United States during the period when many parts of the country were racially segregated by law and by custom. A white patient was rushed into the hospital in distress with cardiac symptoms. The attending physician promptly examined him and ordered the nurse to immediately administer the drug that was the standard protocol in that era. Seeing nothing amiss from her cultural or professional perspective, she just as promptly complies.

Minutes later, another patient is rushed into the hospital with virtually identical symptoms, but he is black. The physician sees him being wheeled in and snaps at the nurse "Send him across town" meaning to a hospital for "negroes," as they would have been called then. "Get him out of here."

The "Negro" hospital was at the other end of town. The nurse judges that the patient's chances of survival would be low if administering the drug is delayed. She now is confronted with a situation in which the first condition isn't met (a fair system) and the order coming from the presiding physician (second condition) although technically legal is likely to result in irreversible harm (third condition unmet).

The nurse now has to decide whether she stands on principle and takes on the whole, unjust system by defiantly treating the patient and vocally demanding the hospital change its policy. Doing so would risk hospital security being called in and her intervention with the patient being forcefully interrupted. Or does she obey the order to remove the patient, risking his life? Which would be more appropriate in this situation—full obedience or outright disobedience? Is there a third, intelligent choice?

What do you think? Once again, we are faced with making a choice that can have irreversible consequences while we are under unforgiving time pressure. What principle do we use?

The principle ethicists might use to answ
toward others and moral inclusion. We admire cc
who stand up for the minority and for the unf.
Instead of disobedience being antisocial, it becon
it is done from the principle of inclusion, rather than

But is it Intelligent Disobedience in this case?

We can argue that civil disobedience at that moment, when the entire culture, institutional structure and onsite authorities would oppose her efforts, would not be in the patient's interest. The goal is to give the patient timely, appropriate treatment to keep his condition from further deteriorating and endangering his life.

With that goal in mind, Intelligent Disobedience in this situation might be to move the patient into a quiet corridor and discreetly administer treatment that would assist the patient's survival until he can be treated at the other hospital. After the event, the nurse would have a different decision to make as to whether she was prepared to challenge the entire system, a challenge of a much larger order of magnitude.

Wise Leaders Value Intelligent Disobedience

Intelligent Disobedience does not imply that the authority figure is acting immorally, though that case certainly occurs. The individual with formal authority may simply be wrong for a variety of reasons. In the case of the emergency room physician, we saw that he may have been too tired to think accurately. There are many other well-intentioned reasons that a person with authority may ask us to do something that is wrong for the situation. By disobeying the specific order, we are not only making an attempt to respond appropriately to the situation, we are also saving authorities from doing things that would harm them or their reputation.

oaching and consulting work, I have repeatedly encoun-
enior executives who are mortified at what they discover is
eing done "because you said so." They may make a casual comment
that is mistaken as a directive to change an operating procedure or a
policy. It makes no sense. It makes operations more difficult. It costs
more money. Yet, it is being done because the authority figure let
out a momentary thought or frustration that was given unexpected
weight—the weight that authority carries in a culture that has not
consciously countered this tendency. These are not even demands by
authority—yet they are implemented.

Mature authority figures recognize that having people around
them capable of and willing to use Intelligent Disobedience is in their
self-interest, as well as in the group's interest. They look for this ability in people they invite into their inner circle. The very best leaders
promote the development of this capacity in all of their people.

Wise Parents Value
Intelligent Disobedience

As I alerted you in the introduction, I am writing to you as the whole
person you are. You may have picked up this book because of a professional imperative for Intelligent Disobedience in your organizational culture. Yet you may also be a parent, grandparent, guardian,
or teacher. The lessons of appropriate obedience and disobedience
are as important or more important in these areas of your life as well.

When an author discusses a book he or she has written or is writing, the author becomes a magnet for stories. Let me share two particularly poignant stories with you. The first is the story of a manager
who took her children to a conference, trying to balance her work and
family life. She was the loving authority figure but, nevertheless, the
authority figure. Therefore, she required obedience from her children.

The time came in the program for her to participate in a presenta-
tion. Her children were too young to reasonably expect them to

accompany her without becoming a distraction. She made sure they would be comfortable in the room, and then impressed on them the need for safety in her absence.

"Under no circumstance are you to leave this room. Do you understand? You are not to open the door for anyone. Do you understand? I need to know that you understand you are not to open the door or to leave the room for any reason."

She left her children, confident of their compliance.

Down in the conference hall the presentations were proceeding smoothly. Her attention was on the proceedings, as they needed to be. Until . . .

A bell started to sound in the conference space. It was not immediately recognized for what it was, so most attendees continued in their conference activities. Then an official ran into the presentation room and shouted, "This is not a drill. There is a fire. Please evacuate now!"

The mother's heart skipped a beat. Her children were on a higher floor in the hotel. She had ordered them under no circumstance to leave the room. UNDER NO CIRUCUMSTANCE!

She rushed out of the presentation room and began pushing her way against the tide of people streaming out of the hotel.

Imagine the panic she must have felt!

Imagine the consequences she feared if her children dutifully obeyed her absolutely strict order! The potential in this situation is almost too tragic to contemplate.

Now, imagine her relief when she saw her two children coming down the stairs as she was rushing up them.

"Mom" they said, "don't get excited. We talked it over and decided that we should not stay in the room when we heard the fire bell."

Take a breath. It is heart stopping for me to even write about this story, told to me by one of the manager's friends and later confirmed by her personally.

The children had pulled a chair to the door so they could look out the security peephole. When they saw the people in the room across the hall leave, they decided they should too. Whether they could articulate this or not, they were operating on a higher value than the value of obedience.

Later in the book we will see stories of young people who did not know when to disobey. For now we can appreciate these children who did.

Let me tell you one more story that makes the point of the life and death potential of even children knowing when and how to intelligently disobey. This is the story of an editor at my publishing house, a very good editor and a very good parent.

He and his family went for a day trip along the winding cliffs of the Pacific Coast Highway. If you have ever driven the stretch of this road between San Francisco and Big Sur in California, you know the dizzying drop-offs that occur at various points and the dramatic vistas of ocean and rocky shore. Sometimes you can see down the steeply sloping hillsides; other times they are too sheer.

Drivers make frequent stops at the scenic overlooks. Occasionally, you get the added treat of spotting seals or other sea mammals. If the fog is out, you see the crashing surf. Always, you hear it. If you get trapped on a low tide beach when the tide reverses, you can be battered against the cliffs and drown.

They had been out of the car for a while and Neal, the dad, felt it was time to move along. He told everyone to get in the car. His kids hesitated. This was a stretch of the road where you could not see what was directly below you on the cliffs. "Dad, we think we hear someone under the cliff calling for help." Neal listened. He couldn't hear anything. "It's probably the wind or a bird," he said. "No, Dad. We heard voices." Neal listened again, straining to hear what they might be interpreting as human voices. "I can't hear anything. Get in the car."

The kids refused to obey. "No, Dad. You need to call someone to help."

With great reservation that he would be wasting the highway patrol's time, Neal phoned, reported their location and the fact that his kids insisted they heard someone calling for help. The kids further insisted that they wait to be sure the patrol knew the right spot. This was disobedience bordering on a "sit in" demonstration.

The highway patrol arrived with the equipment needed for search and rescue. It did not take long for them to locate the stranded hikers at the foot of the cliff. How proud Neal was that his children had refused to obey. How chastened he was that he had almost overridden them.

Developing the Right Balance

These are stories of appropriate disobedience with positive endings. As we will see, there are many stories in which individuals did not overcome the weight of authority and the expectation of obedience.

The emergency room nurse, like the children in these stories, somehow acquired a sufficiently strong internal values compass so that, without professional preparation for the intensity of the moment, she was able to intelligently disobey. As we continue our examination of this subject, we will see that, despite our belief in our own goodness and intelligence, we cannot be certain that we would have disobeyed in the heat of the moment with the weight of authority demanding we do as we are told. We need to learn how to get the balance right between the appropriate obedience all cultures and legitimate authorities have a right to expect and the timely use of Intelligent Disobedience when we are asked to do something we believe is harmful.

We can extract several fundamentals of Intelligent Disobedience from this chapter:

1. As distinct from civil disobedience, Intelligent Disobedience works within a system rather than challenging the system itself.

2. While acknowledging the legitimacy of authorities within that system, Intelligent Disobedience evaluates the morality

and workability of specific orders received from those authorities and acts accordingly.

3. Intelligent Disobedience references a set of values held by the individual or the society that take precedence over a specific order.

4. Once the order has been weighed against the higher values, a decision is made and appropriate action is taken.

5. After Intelligent Disobedience has been used to avoid the potential harm in a specific situation, a deeper examination of the system itself may be performed.

6. Leaders who value good outcomes more than assertion of their own authority understand that serious errors are avoided by the use of Intelligent Disobedience.

7. Parents, teachers, and caregivers will encounter expressions of Intelligent Disobedience.

8. By recognizing and honoring these acts, they prevent regrettable outcomes, build confidence in the youth who are in their care, and affirm the merits of Intelligent Disobedience.

CHAPTER THREE

Breaking the Habit:
It Takes More than You Think

M Y WORK ON INTELLIGENT DISOBEDIENCE is a natural out-growth of my earlier work on courageous followers. Courageous followers form relationships with their leaders in which they are both supportive of the leader and willing to give the leader candid feedback on the impact of the leader's actions. For those interested, there is an overview of the topic in the appendix.

I was in Los Angeles giving a presentation on courageous followership at the International Leadership Association. ILA is an interesting group that was formed to bring together scholars, educators, and practitioners of leadership so they can enrich one another's work in the field. I have since become a member of the ILA's board of directors, but then I was simply a conference attendee and presenter.

After my presentation, a former army officer introduced himself to me and began telling one of the most fascinating stories I had ever heard on how to *break the habit* of too much obedience to authority. I'll share that story with you in a minute. I promised to say a little more about courageous followership, so let me do that first.

In some cultures, such as in the United States, tremendous value is placed on being a leader. Anyone who applies to college, for example, knows that you are asked to list all the leadership roles you have played. It can make high school students frantic if they are aiming for admission to competitive schools. They run around trying to be the captain of the team of their spring sport and captain of their fall sport, president of this student group and that student council, and leader of a couple of outside volunteer groups on top of it. Do these same college applications ever ask about roles in which you have provided excellent support to a leader? They do not.

Yet, what is the one thing a leader needs in order to lead? The answer: *a follower*. If no one is following, then no matter how brilliant the individual may be, he or she is not leading. If it is the follower who makes the individual into a leader, why is it that only the leader role is honored?

It turns out that the answer to this is at least partly explained by our culture labeling "follower" as a personality type. Just as validly, and often more validly, "follower" can be thought of as a *role*. If the captain of the baseball team and the basketball team also likes to play hockey, he knows he doesn't also have to lead the hockey team. He doesn't have the time and energy for that additional role and maybe also lacks the skill. So he gives his support to the hockey team captain and becomes a strong follower in that situation. If he could never follow anyone he would, in fact, be a disruptive presence on the team.

Looked at in this way, being in the follower role is not a sign of weakness. Think about it. Is a vice principal a follower or a leader? The answer: she is both. Is the school principal a follower or a leader? She had better be both. If she doesn't lead, her school will suffer. If she can't follow, the county administrator of schools will become frustrated with her, and the principal will have less influence in contributing to the administrator's thinking and planning.

The correct question is not whether it is okay to play a follower role, but *How can I play the follower role with integrity and strength*? Courageous followership explores the ways to build a strong relationship with leaders that becomes a *partnership*. Partners support one another in their mutual efforts to succeed. They respect one another's agreed on roles in the partnership. They also talk honestly about what the other is doing that could interfere with success, even if one is in a junior role to the other.

That very brief description of courageous followership brings us back to the ex-army officer's story. A courageous follower speaks "truth to power" regardless of whether the leader invites him or her to do so. But a smart leader knows there are very strong social forces at work that inhibit the person in the follower role from speaking candidly. This is similar to the situation with the service dog we looked at in the last chapter. A lot of training has occurred to ensure obedience. What does it now take to break the habit when it would be unsafe to follow an order?

The former serviceman who approached me in Los Angeles gives us a vivid illustration of just how much it can take to break the obedience habit. Note carefully: we are not interested in weakening obedience to the legitimate, ethical, and productive uses of authority. After all, this is the military, which even more than other institutions relies on an agreed upon use of authority. We are talking about transforming the habit into a conscious choice of whether to obey or to dissent in a specific situation.

At the time, the officer was a young lieutenant. You can picture him stationed at one of the large army bases scattered around the United States. They are worlds unto themselves, stretching for many square miles inside a fenced perimeter. The soldiers train and work there. The married soldiers' families live there. It's the soil they deploy from on overseas missions and return to when their difficult missions are complete. Everyone on the base knows his or her rank relative to everyone else on the base. Breaches of protocol are taken seriously. Reputations are formed and tend to stick. You don't step out of line lightly. This is the story he told me.

At the time I was working for a captain who had a rigid, authoritarian style. I reported every morning for my daily orders. He always had a list of the ten things he wanted done. If I mentioned there was something else that needed doing that day that wasn't on the list, his gruff response was "You do the ten things on my list and then you can do yours."

Note that the item on the lieutenant's list may have been more important to the base than all the items on the captain's list. The captain couldn't care less. What was important to him was his authority and your compliance with it. Fortunately, this lieutenant had enough commitment to the base and to his fellow soldiers that he got the eleventh thing done anyway, which at times was the true priority. By doing so, he probably saved the captain from looking bad to his own superiors without the captain ever knowing or acknowledging it. Given the captain's total insistence on obedience, things might have worked out very differently to the detriment of everyone concerned.

> *Eventually, the captain rotated out and a new captain took his place. I reported as usual the morning of the new captain's arrival. After a few pleasantries, the captain gave me an order that he wanted done that day. I said, "Yes, sir!, saluted, and turned to leave.*
>
> *As I was facing the door, I heard the captain say, "Hold on a minute." I swiveled around and the next thing he said took me by surprise, to say the least. "Did the order I just gave make sense to you?"*
>
> *Naturally, I replied, "Yes, sir!" He paused and fixed his eyes on me. "Did it really make sense to you?" he repeated.*
>
> *Suddenly, I was in a very awkward situation. Did the captain's order really make sense to me? The directness of his question and intensity in his voice wouldn't let me fudge an answer. I had to admit to myself that I wasn't sure if it made sense.*

What was going on in the lieutenant's mind? Of course, he didn't want to start off on the wrong foot with his new superior officer. So his mind started jumping through the social calculations of the effect of different answers he might give, just one of the ways that differences in rank can distort the natural flow of communication. More problematically, how is it that this bright, willing young officer wasn't sure if the order made sense to him, yet he was leaving to execute it anyway? That's a deeper level of internal self-deception, disowning his own accountability for acting rationally and responsibly. Right here we have a window into the mechanism that has at times allowed otherwise decent military, law enforcement, and intelligence personnel to commit acts that violate the standards of their profession and human decency.

Apparently, the lieutenant had been so conditioned by the last captain's "no-thinking-for-yourself" style that his power to judge the sense of an order had gone into a state of suspension. It had caused him to move further along the spectrum from a rational and responsible individual to the state we instinctively fear—that of the automaton. The automaton seems to be acting on its own but is actually following a programmed set of instructions for which it is not responsible. In the human version, because the individual is implementing a strict set of instructions given by another individual with formal authority, they do not *feel* responsible. We are right to fear this disassociation from self-accountability.

In the lieutenant's case, the last captain's order was just the most extreme expression of the expectation of unquestioned obedience. Whoever heard of a superior officer asking the question *Did the order I just gave make sense to you*? The lieutenant was so used to obeying orders in general, and obeying the last captain's orders to the letter, that he hadn't given conscious thought to the content of the particular order he had just received. A dangerous state of affairs for anyone, but particularly for military personnel trusted with high-powered armament and national honor and security.

The captain, for his part, had set up the lieutenant. The order he had given really didn't make sense. It was a test to see if he could trust his subordinate to exercise sufficiently independent thinking to question the order. If the lieutenant questioned the order, the captain would be able to trust him. If the lieutenant blindly tried to execute the order, the captain would have a concrete, real-time example to help expose the habit to the lieutenant himself.

What did the lieutenant do?

I said something to the effect of "Sir, the order may not have been fully clear to me given our current situation." As I said this, I realized I had doubts about the wisdom of the order, given the context in which it would be executed.

"Lieutenant," the captain said in a very serious tone. "I cannot afford to have you go off and execute something in my name if you are not clear what the order is or if, from your knowledge of the situation on the ground, you do not think it is a smart thing to do."

I said, "Yes, sir!" thinking that would be the end of the matter. But the captain wasn't ready to let it go.

He said, "We're going to practice how to deal with the situation if what I tell you doesn't make sense."

This is a crucial juncture. The new captain, having witnessed the lieutenant's conditioning to please and obey, recognized that this last "Yes, sir!" was just one more expression of that conditioning. In itself, it was not a meaningful demonstration of the lieutenant's capacity to "unlearn" the conditioning.

Unlearning the habit was going to take some work. We don't know from this story where the captain developed his appreciation for the need to break the mindless obedience habit. Perhaps he had a mentor who helped him break it. Perhaps he saw the consequences of unthinking obedience earlier in his career and was determined to never let that occur again on his watch.

The captain then told me: "I'm going to give you an order that doesn't make any sense and you're going to tell me 'That's BS, sir.' "

I couldn't believe what I was hearing! This was the army. No one said "that's BS" to a superior officer without predictable and unpleasant consequences.

I said "Sir, I can't say that."

The captain told me, "Yes, you can" and proceeded to give me an order that wasn't well thought out and could have pretty negative consequences.

I didn't want to disobey the order to tell him that was BS, so I said as softly as I could—in sort of a whisper, "That's BS, sir."

We're witnessing a clever piece of habit-breaking ju-jitsu here. The captain was trying to break the habit of mindless disobedience. This same programming to obey would allow the junior office to break with his conditioning so he could practice telling his superior that his order was BS. He had been given a direct order to do so!

The captain heard me and said, "Alright, now let's try that again a little louder. I had to do this over and over until I could say "That's BS, sir!" as effectively as I could say "Yes, sir!" when responding to reasonable orders.

The captain was applying the techniques of good training. Repeat the skill being learned until it can be performed with confidence and strength.

Several weeks went by. Each morning I reported and received my orders, careful to make sure I understood them and could responsibly execute them. Everything was going fine. Then one morning I reported to the captain and found the colonel in the office with him. Here's where it got really interesting.

The colonel had a nephew who was also stationed on the base. Apparently, the nephew had taken a military vehicle without authorization. The military police had caught him, and the colonel had come to the captain to see if they could work out something to get his nephew off the hook. The captain explained to me what they were trying to do and asked for my help.

This was the moment of truth for the lieutenant. Would he revert to the safety of his primary training to obediently comply? The presence of the colonel raised the stakes. His own superior understood the need for candor from his troops, but did the colonel? Was this a time to apply the new training the captain had insisted on giving him? Note that the lieutenant had moved from mindless obedience to being aware that he had a choice in the matter. This is the primary condition for intelligent disobedience. He made his choice.

> "Sir, that's BS, sir." And I said it in a clear, strong voice.
>
> The colonel went nuts. His eyes bulged. His eyebrows shot up. His face turned red. There was a look of astonishment on it. He pointed a trembling finger at me and stammered in a loud voice: "What . . . what did he just say!?"
>
> For me it was a surreal moment. The colonel looked like he was going to explode. I froze. Fortunately, the captain had the presence of mind to intervene. He took a step to place himself between me and the colonel. He raised his arm toward the colonel, sort of like he was a blocker using a stiff arm to protect the runner from a tackle. He said in an equally strong voice, "It's alright sir. I'll take care of this."
>
> He took a couple of quick steps toward me, put his arm around my shoulder, and sort of hustled me out of the room. As he did so he said softly, "Well done. You did well." And then, after another couple of steps he continued to say softly, "Now get out of here before the colonel kills you!"

The lieutenant passed the test. This was not another set up by the captain to see if the lieutenant would obey when he shouldn't. This was the real thing. The captain, who should have known better, fell into the cultural trap of obeying his superior officer when he shouldn't have. We're all human. Fortunately, the training he had given the lieutenant at the outset of their relationship saved the captain from going down the unethical road with its potential consequences to everyone involved. The lieutenant had been inculcated with an alternate response to blind obedience. This had permitted him to break the personal and culturally expected habit to obey.

Then the captain took the opportunity to do something critical: reward and thus reinforce the behavior. Imagine if he had been critical of the lieutenant for having spoken up in front of the colonel. This, most likely and understandably, would have undermined the lieutenant's willingness to disobey an ill-advised order in the future. If we need our team to exercise Intelligent Disobedience, and I think you'll agree that we do, then we need to be consistent in rewarding its display and certainly avoid penalizing it.

Did the captain have to be so dramatic in training the lieutenant to say, "That's BS!"? Couldn't he have trained him instead to respectfully question the order? Sure. And that probably would have worked, too. But perhaps the outrageousness of telling your superior officer "That's BS!" more radically broke through the thick neural connections that years of conditioning had developed. It would, of course, be healthy for the lieutenant to develop a wider repertoire of how to question or dissent. "That's BS" was the fire-axe that broke the chains of obedience. The axe could still be kept in reserve, while a finer tool kit was acquired that served the same purpose with less risk of eye-popping fireworks!

We also hope that the lieutenant passed on this coaching to the noncommissioned officers who reported to him and they, in turn, to the enlisted soldiers. I did not, at the time, have the presence to inquire about this. That would be how a culture is changed.

Let's review the elements we saw at work here that were required to break the cultural habit. Clearly, it is not simply a matter of saying "We value candor here," which would have been completely inadequate to changing behavior. We can summarize the elements as follows:

1. Create an awareness of the existing habit of obedience. None of us likes to think of ourselves as being blindly obedient so it may take catching us in the act of doing so to create the awareness needed to change.

2. Create awareness of the negative value of unquestioning obedience. Many have been raised to value obedience and

do not recognize under what circumstances obedience is no longer appropriate or expected.

3. Impress on those you lead that you will not reward blind obedience and you will not penalize Intelligent Disobedience.

4. Provide alternative responses to blind obedience. Clarify what responses would be acceptable, preferred, desired, even rewarded.

5. Practice the alternative responses to blind obedience. Firefighters practice running into burning buildings under controlled conditions before the sudden need to do the real thing.

6. Practice until Intelligent Disobedience can be performed with a strong voice. This isn't just reading from a script—it requires projection to make the needed impact.

7. Commend the use of Intelligent Disobedience when it occurs. Do you really want principled dissent? This is the moment of truth when your credibility is tested and found to be trustworthy or not.

8. Protect the subordinate who displays appropriate disobedience. Not everyone will share your commitment to Intelligent Disobedience. Make sure those who share your commitment don't pay a price for their trust in you.

We will examine these elements further as we look at how they have been applied in high-risk situations.

CHAPTER FOUR

Finding Your Voice:
Saying "No" So You Are Heard

IN THE LAST CHAPTER, we heard the captain coaching the lieutenant to use a level of voice that would convey his assessment of the situation. If we use too weak a voice, we don't make enough impact to be taken seriously. If we use too strong a voice, we can be written off as rude, arrogant, or even threatening. Guide dogs are discouraged from barking a warning because doing so frightens people around them.

What is your effective level of voice? Is it always the same, or does it depend on the situation that you are questioning? Is it governed by your personality or by conscious choices you can make? Why is clarifying and grasping this important to Intelligent Disobedience?

In its simplest form, disobedience is receiving an order and either saying "no" you won't do that, skipping the verbal response and just not doing it, or willfully doing something different than you were told. Any of these may be an effective response in specific situations but not necessarily a socially intelligent act.

Intelligent Disobedience adds additional dimensions to your response. First of all, in many cases you still need to live with or work for the person who issued the order. Because this person has a degree of formal authority, if he labels your response insubordination, that can affect your status or progress in ways you would rather avoid.

Second, in some situations it is not enough to simply disobey if executing the order would be dangerous. The person in authority can still take the action directly if he has not comprehended the danger, or he can give the order to someone else to execute who is either not aware of the danger or who is less willing to disobey. Therefore, Intelligent

Disobedience almost always involves communicating effectively why you are questioning or disobeying the order you have received.

That brings us back to the subject of voice. To examine this, we're going to look at situations in which using the right voice to warn superiors of danger they are failing to see, or failing to correctly estimate, can mean the difference between life and death.

The Guide Dog and Voice

Let's first go back to the dog in the preface that is sitting patiently under the desk of the woman training him. In this case, the dog is being groomed to support individuals who have lost, or never had, vision. There are other types of service dogs that have received similar training to support individuals with different needs, for example people who have lost their hearing or who are diabetic and in danger of going into a diabetic coma. Depending on what type of role the service dog has been selected and trained for, it has to find its "voice" for Intelligent Disobedience. The higher level trainer whom the initial trainer sends the dog to next will help develop that voice.

The effective voice will depend on two things: what the dog finds most natural and what the leader—the human whom the dog is supporting—needs. The expert trainer will learn the dog's natural temperament and inclinations and build its "voice" around existing strengths.

It will, however, do no good for a dog employed as a hearing dog to alert the leader by barking if the leader lacks the capacity to hear. If the dog is employed as a guide dog to compensate for visual impairment, the leader can hear, though warning by insistent barking or growling may confuse the leader and alarm passersby who do not understand what the dog is doing. A different way of effectively warning the leader must be learned.

Let's take the case of the guide dog first. The dog is trained to follow the human's commands such as "forward," "stop," "right," "left," and so forth. It is the leader who determines the direction and destination. They practice this together so the dog comes to know the goal. Once they are on the move, it is the dog's responsibility to make sure they get there safely.

What could get in their way? All sorts of things. Construction can be causing the need for detours. Painting or window cleaning can produce ground-level or head-level obstructions. A delivery to a shop storage room can result in open cellar doors. After winter storms, snow plows may have created large ice barriers at crosswalks. Cars may come around corners quickly before the leader who gives the command to go forward hears the approach.

In each of these cases, the guide dog must not obey the command to go forward. And it must do so firmly enough that the leader halts in time to avoid injuring the team (human and dog). The guide dog's "voice" is transmitted in unambiguous body "language" through the handle that is connecting the team.

Recognize that in this situation the leader does not know immediately what is the danger. A trust has grown within the team that if the dog refuses to obey a command, or ceases executing the command, there is a reason for doing so. If the dog stays paused, the leader must too, until she grasps the nature of the danger and can give an alternate command like "Find another way," which guide dogs are trained to do. If the dog determines it would be dangerous to stay in the current position and assertively pulls the leader in a different direction, the leader needs to trust her partner and follow.

Neither the dog nor the human can afford for the dog to give ambiguous signals in these situations. Clarity is critical. Equally critical is the leader's response. There are two important responses. The first of course is for the leader to follow without hesitation. For the moment, be the one who is led. The second, perhaps less obvious, is to thank and reward the dog for having taken an action to protect the team. The literature on Intelligent Disobedience in service dog training shows that if the behavior is not rewarded, it will deteriorate over time. Sound familiar?

The Human Voice:
Speaking Up to Command

Let's compare these lessons to human situations and see what transfers. Human "voice" has a much greater range. How is this tool best used when disobedience may be called for?

The simplest situation is when there is strong potential for serious harm if the order is carried out. The dedication to my book *The Courageous Follower* contains an example of this. A soldier was ordered to fire on a specific target. He had strong reason to believe that the indicated target were actually our own soldiers. He reported this and refused the order, even when it was repeated. A subsequent investigation of the incident proved he was right. Instead of being disciplined, he was awarded a medal for his courage to disobey a wrong order. He had to take as firm a stand in that situation as the guide dog who refuses to go forward when there is a newly excavated pit in front of the team.

This may be a simple situation in terms of the "voice" required, but it is not an easy situation. The soldier needed a lot of confidence in his own perceptions. If he had misperceived the situation and disobeyed the order, his refusal to take out the enemy position may have had deadly consequences for other soldiers. If he had not trusted his own perceptions and fired on the target, his obedience would have likely resulted in the death of fellow soldiers. We see how critical it is to maintain what is known as situational awareness and to be responsible for what we see and for how we respond.

What about when we are not sure we are interpreting the situation correctly? Does this relieve us of responsibility? Or do we have to find different levels of voice to help us and our leaders better assess potential dangers before committing to a course of action? Professionalism and common sense tell us we should still be responsible. How do we go about doing that?

For examples of this, we can turn to the aviation industry. In the 1970s and early 1980s, there were a number of deadly airline crashes.

These each involved scores or hundreds of fatalities, the worst resulting in 583 deaths when two jumbo jets collided on a takeoff maneuver. Although there are many more deaths annually in automobile accidents, the large numbers of deaths usually involved in a single aviation accident attract a lot of media coverage. The aviation industry knows that it needs to keep accidents to the smallest number possible or many people, seeing accident media coverage, would choose not to fly. It is, therefore, in both the travelers' and the industry's interest to do what is necessary to find the source of accidents and eliminate or minimize them. As a result, there is a well-developed investigation apparatus. In the United States, it takes the form of the National Transportation Safety Board. After each accident, protocols are vigorously implemented to identify its causes and generate remedies to prevent future accidents from similar causes.

A key finding of these investigations was that breakdown in communication among the crew, or between the crew and the flight control tower, was a major cause of avoidable accidents. Many factors go into successful communication and into eliminating the barriers to achieve this. Several of these apply to the practice of Intelligent Disobedience.

We must remember that on commercial airplanes there are two certified pilots, but only one, the captain, is in command. The role of captain on a ship or airplane holds tremendous accountability and imposing authority. In addition, many commercial pilots come to civil aviation from the military, so respect for command is well established. Habitual deference to command can create a bias to agree with command's perceptions, to refrain from questioning those perceptions, or to questioning them too timidly to make a difference. Think of the lieutenant in the prior story before his retraining.

The following is an excerpt from the transcript of the final minutes of Air Florida Flight 90 before it crashed into the Potomac River in Washington, DC. It was an icy winter day in 1982, and the plane, after delays on the runway due to a series of unusual occurrences, had not been adequately de-iced before the takeoff procedure began. The engine instruments were not reading in the necessary range to properly accomplish the takeoff. The pilot misinterpreted the reading as instrument error and discounted the data he was being given by the instruments. Note the first officer's voice and how he tones down his concern when, instead, he should hold firm or become more assertive.

Taken from cockpit voice recorder:

First officer: *God, look at this thing. That doesn't seem right, does it? Uh, that's not right.*

Captain: *Yes it is, there's eighty.*

First officer: *Naw, I don't think that's right. Ah, maybe it is.*

Captain: *Hundred and twenty.*

First officer: *I don't know.*

Captain: *Vee-one. Easy, vee-two.*

(Sound of stick shaker starts and continues until impact 22 seconds later.)

The only other time we hear the first officer's voice is one second before impact when he says, "Larry, we're going down, Larry. . . ."

The captain says, "I know it" at the moment of the crash. Everyone aboard dies, except four passengers who are pulled from the icy river.

Mitigating Language

What was going on with the first officer? Linguists have a term for how he muted his concerns; they call it *mitigating language*. It is deferential or indirect language that is used between people by the person with less formal power.

Mitigating language can be helpful in managing social and professional relations when used deliberately in situations that are not urgent or still ambiguous. Rather than sound like an alarmist or a know-it-all, you can consciously use mitigating language to draw attention to what may be a problem.

> *"I'm not sure if we need to be concerned, but I noticed . . ."*
> *"I know I'm new here, but I wondered if* _____ *is the way it should be?"*

In nonurgent or ambiguous situations, you can begin with mitigating language and then escalate your concern if you do not receive a response that adequately addresses the potential risk. In situations where it is clear that there is a high degree of risk, mitigating language is very dangerous.

Notice that the first officer started off with an assertive statement:

> *"God, look at this thing. That doesn't seem right, does it? Uh, that's not right."*

When the captain disagreed and said "Yes it is," instead of escalating his language, the first officer backed down and began using mitigating language.

> *"Naw, I don't think that's right. Ah, maybe it is."*

His trained deference to authority kicked in, with disastrous results.

Robert Baron, president of The Aviation Consulting Group, which specializes in human factors training, gave the following assessment of the Air Florida's first officer's failure to use the appropriate level of voice:

> *"What the first officer should have done was voice his concerns in a more assertive fashion (as the message sender, his message was not being received). Typically, if something does not look right by the pilot not flying (in this case the first officer) an "abort" callout*

should be made and the pilot flying (in this case the Captain)
should unquestionably abort the takeoff."[1]

Baron is identifying that the correct behavior would have been Intelligent Disobedience through the use of the appropriate level of voice. The captain, implicitly or explicitly, expected the first officer to go along with his assessment of the situation. Instead, the first officer should have ordered an abort as clearly as the guide dog that blocks the vision-impaired handler from stepping off a curb in front of an oncoming automobile.

What does it take to overcome a lifetime of deference to authority in order to exert the appropriate level of voice? The answer: *practice the behavior*!

In many of the fatal airline accidents, the investigation found that vague or insufficiently assertive language by subordinate officers was a significant factor in the disaster. The impulse to remain silent, speak deferentially, and allow the captain to continue to put the aircraft in harm's way had to be transformed!

A new level of training was needed.

Crew Resource Management

Human factor training emerged from a study done in 1979 by the National Aeronautic and Space Agency (NASA) into the nontechnical causes contributing to fatal airline crashes. United Airlines was the first to implement what came to be known as CRM training. Initially, CRM stood for Cockpit Resource Management. It was expanded to include the cabin crew and became known as Crew Resource Management. The aim: make use of *all* the crew resources to improve safety.

CRM-trained crews were better prepared to detect and deal with safety problems while they were still manageable. Versions of CRM were soon adopted by all major civil airlines and then modified to meet military aviation needs. The incidence of major airline crashes reduced significantly. Over the decades that CRM training has been in existence, it has naturally evolved. Different organizations and nationalities have adapted it to fit their own cultures. All emphasize better communication among crew members of all ranks and the reduction or containment of errors. The training includes simulations that allow the crew to practice the desirable behaviors so they are prepared to use them in real world situations that occur unexpectedly.

The skill sets developed in CRM training that most directly apply to Intelligent Disobedience can be summarized as follows:

◆ All participants must maintain situational awareness.

◆ When a crew member sees an anomaly—a condition out of the ordinary—he must pay attention to determine if the condition may pose a risk to the flight.

◆ If there is a potential risk, the crew member must draw it to the captain's attention with sufficient assertiveness to get him to focus on the situation.

◆ The captain in different simulations may be distracted by checklist items, by personal thoughts, by conversation, or may simply not appreciate the extent of risk.

◆ The crew member must increase the level of assertiveness until the captain is giving the situation appropriate attention and taking situation-appropriate action.

From this, we recognize that the army captain in the last chapter was conducting his own form of CRM training with the lieutenant. The lieutenant's willingness and ability to speak assertively to the captain was not personality based—it had been shaped through lifelong socialization. The capacity to rise above his conditioning in order to speak assertively when warranted was recognized by the captain as an important and valued behavior, which he helped the lieutenant develop through simulated practice.

The army captain and lieutenant were new to each other and needed to establish a way of quickly lowering the risk of obeying unwise orders. Similarly, flight crews rotate and mix and match, so training in expected standards of assertive voice is critical. They do not have the luxury of time in which to learn one another's more subtle signals.

The willingness for junior flight officers to speak with sufficient assertiveness is further complicated by the value placed on deference to authority in different cultures. The more value a culture places on authority, the more important it is to find ways of overriding the tendency for subordinates to remain silent or to speak ineffectively in high-risk situations, without fearing they are causing the authority to "lose face" or retaliate.

One of the ways to do this is to characterize all errors as a group responsibility rather than as the responsibility of the leader. Cultures that are high in deference to authority also tend to place more value on collective welfare and action than on individual freedom and responsibility. Training can focus on all members of the team using adequate voice to ensure the group's safety and well-being. Harking back to the service dog model, the exercise of Intelligent Disobedience implies no criticism and is solely done to protect the team from harm.

Error and risk can never be fully eliminated. Even with CRM training, fatal crashes due to human error occur. Nevertheless, the incidence of major airline disasters has significantly reduced after the adoption of CRM. It is a proven model that can be modified and adapted to other environments. Recently, it has been one of the models from which improved surgical room procedures have been developed. Before a surgery begins, every member of the surgical team, regardless of status within the medical hierarchy, must vocally give their assent to the procedure beginning and to it concluding. A nod of the head is insufficient. There is recognition of the need for clear language to overcome the social forces of hierarchy and to enroll personal accountability. This has reduced the number of "hospital errors" that have plagued otherwise respected institutions.

Poet David Whyte, in his unusual and moving book, *The Heart Aroused: Poetry and the Preservation of the Soul in Corporate America*,[2] displays a poet's appreciation of the power of language. He tells the story of an executive, the highest authority in the room, who demands that all his subordinates around the table express their support for his proposed plan on a scale of 1 to 10, 10 being full, enthusiastic support. Those around the table had discussed the plan among themselves and concluded it contained far more risk than warranted. But lacking the courage to voice their disagreement, each in turn vocally gave the plan a 10. When it was the last manager's turn, he desperately wanted to give it a 1 or 2 to force a discussion of the risks involved. When he opened his mouth, what came out was 9. Instead of roaring his disagreement like a lion, he could only squeak it like a mouse, *but at least it was a start.*

Sometimes you will only be able to muster the courage to use mitigating language to voice your concern. But when the risks are great and the window for reducing them narrow, you must be prepared to find the courage of the lion. Maybe not a roar, but at least a firm "Wait! I need your attention! You are missing a significant danger in this situation."

You must generate enough presence in your intelligent dissent to require the leader to reassess before moving forward. Airline crews and hospital surgical teams are required to practice this. If you can create these practice opportunities in your organization, you should do so. If not, you may need to practice them yourself so the full power of your voice is available when needed. A lot—sometimes everything—may depend on it.

A simple exercise you or your team can do is to imagine a situation in which a decision is about to be made by people who outrank you. You believe there is significant risk that has not been accounted for in their thinking. Practice consciously bringing this risk to their attention in language that begins as mitigating and increases in assertiveness as needed. This is to help you get clarity on the difference between the types of language. Vocalize simple sentences designed to do this. Examples of these follow.

I know I am new and I may not have all the information, but I am wondering if we need to consider some risks that may exist? (highly mitigating)

I may not have made my point well so let me try again: I wonder if we have considered the risks associated with _____? (mitigating)

Based on what I am hearing, I am concerned that _____ contains risks that warrant a discussion before we proceed. (mildly assertive)

Given the information we have, this approach contains a serious risk that we need to overcome before proceeding. (assertive)

We need to alter our course now before we do irreversible damage. (insistently assertive)

When we cycle back to the socialization of our youth in classrooms, in religious education, in after-school activities, we will need to address how and when to introduce age-appropriate versions of voice in questioning authority. For the moment, thinking once more as a whole person, begin to pay attention to how you as a parent, a teacher, a coach model appropriate voice in speaking to children, to other adults, to the authority figures with whom you interact, inside and outside the workplace.

Remember these principles:

1. Intelligent obedience and Intelligent Disobedience usually involve spoken or written language, as well as the act itself.

2. We each have a learned voice we have acquired to navigate social and hierarchical situations that serves us well in certain situations.

3. We need to become aware of that learned voice in terms of where it falls on the scale of mitigating-to-assertive language so we can make conscious choices about using the voice appropriate to a situation.

4. By practicing the choice of which voice to use in different situations, we become better prepared to use an appropriate voice when needed and to adjust our voice further as warranted for our communication to be effective.

5. Each of us has unique speech patterns that are natural to us; we can adapt the principles of mitigating and assertive language to what feels comfortable to us and is effective for the situation.

6. These skills are important both for teams that continuously work together and for teams that frequently shift their composition, so that all team members recognize an assertive voice as a safety warning rather than as a threat.

7. Cultures that are very high in deference must give these skills extra attention to ensure every group member will speak up and be heard when it is necessary to protect the group and those served by the group.

8. If you cannot speak as assertively as you would like, at least speak so the leader and group have a chance to consider the potential danger you see.

9. Vocalizing a concern is not sufficient when Intelligent Disobedience requires an action, but we should still vocalize our concerns, except in the most immediate situation requiring split-second action.

CHAPTER FIVE

Understanding the True Risks of Saying "Yes"

BY THIS POINT YOU MAY BE QUESTIONING, and perhaps should be questioning, the analogy I have chosen between guide dogs and human beings. When a guide dog exercises Intelligent Disobedience, it is in the face of an immediate threat—stepping in front of a car, falling into a sinkhole, getting entangled with a downed electric wire. Aren't responses to immediate threats simpler than responses to longer term potential dangers or to morally complex situations?

If the highest ranking person in your school or organization was about to step in front of a moving car, you wouldn't hesitate to yell "Be careful!" or even to yank him back by the arm. The official you saved from injury or worse is also likely to have a grateful response of "Thank you!" Nothing very complex here: someone is in sudden danger and you display an instinctive response, which is appreciated. So is this metaphor helpful in more complex situations in which the senior official might not share your assessment of the risks?

I think it is in a couple of ways. Let's explore those.

The Suddenness of a Situation

Here is an example from a federal agency press conference. People don't die from press conferences. The conference had been scheduled with short notice and was due to start. Press conferences are typically held to get out an organization's message, to shape an issue in the public mind, and to make the organization and its leaders look good. Instead, this press conference made the organization and its leader look bad. Very bad. And it did so because, in the crunch of the moment, there was an absence of Intelligent Disobedience.

The press conference announcement went out too late to attract the desired media presence. A reasonable choice in a situation like this would have been to announce that the conference was rescheduled for a later date. Instead, some bright spark had a more clever idea. The agency's public affairs staff were ordered to fill the seats in the briefing room usually occupied by members of the media and to ask questions of the agency head as if they were actual credentialed press.

The number of ways in which this order was issued in poor judgment is hard to count. The primary requisite of good leadership is to build trust with those it serves; therefore, the primary requisite of the organization's public affairs office must be to support building that trust and to resist any effort that would undermine trust. Ordering public affairs staff to engage in a blatant deception is asking them to compromise the reputation for integrity on which their relationships with the media rest. On top of that, the professional press corps in any city or industry is a fairly tight group who know one another well. It is inconceivable that any genuinely credentialed press person in the room wouldn't recognize the deception or, in this age where everything is videoed, that someone viewing the press conference a few hours later wouldn't look with incredulity at government employees posing as independent media. Yet, the order was given.

Let's put ourselves in the shoes of the public affairs staff receiving the order. We're focused on whatever our priorities are that day. We have a list of things that need doing, calls to be made, statements to be drafted, research to be done.

Suddenly, our direct supervisor bursts in and says something like

"Folks, we have an emergency. No one has showed up for the press conference and the Administrator [that's the top dog in a federal agency] *is due to speak in five minutes. We can't fizzle out on this one. Get down to the briefing room and sit in the reporters' seats! A couple of you think of some questions to toss him. Nothing too*

tough. Hurry up, please. He's really hot about this! I've got to get back to him now!"

Our supervisor rushes out of the room.

We're all somewhat stunned. Nothing like this has ever happened before. Our professional instincts tell us this is wrong. But by the very nature of such an order—lacking precedents, the urgency with which it was delivered, and the fact that this involves the big boss himself—our judgment is temporarily overwhelmed and we experience confusion. Maybe this really is important enough to do? When we see a couple of our colleagues grab their notebooks and head out the door to the briefing room, we hesitantly but dutifully follow.

Nobody's life was at stake in the phony media situation. The agency, however, was severely embarrassed when the story made headlines in widely read, legitimate media. The agency administrator hemmed and hawed through explanations of what had occurred and lost significant standing in his professional community. The public affairs personnel involved had smears on their reputation that would take a long time to live down.

This is a real, if absurd example in its lack of judgment. At times, orders that will produce more harm than good are thrown at us suddenly. It is precisely at those moments when we are stunned by the instructions being issued that we need the mental strength and discipline to slow things down while we rationally process the situation and choices.

This brings us to that mouthful of a topic: cognitive dissonance. What does this psychological jargon mean?

When we believe something and then are confronted with evidence that what we believe may not be true, our brain struggles to reconcile the dissonance between these incompatible states. Usually, it will do so in favor of the earlier held belief. How? By sweeping the new data under the proverbial rug, considering it "not credible," devaluing it, and creating clever rationalizations for how the original belief *must* still be valid. Dissonance is not pleasant. It is unharmonious, lacks accord, and jangles the nerves.

Our impulse is to reduce the uncomfortable dissonance. We most often do so by rationalizing away the conflicting new data. Instead, we need to stay alert for the signs of dissonance and allow ourselves to experience it. Only by tolerating dissonance, and vigilantly exploring why it seems to be occurring, will we allow ourselves to reach an answer on which we can take a principled stand.

Whether a guide dog chooses to let the human step off the curb or not, there is no do-over. It is better to pause firmly until the team can assess the risk than to succumb to cognitive dissonance and rationalize it away.

> **Cognitive dissonance:** Dog knows cars make noise, the electric vehicle coming around the corner isn't making noise, it's probably not a car, therefore it doesn't go against my training to stop for oncoming cars, I should follow my training, we can step off the curb. Splat!

> **Overriding cognitive dissonance:** Cars make noise, the object coming isn't making noise, still it is coming. I'll make us stop until we figure out what it is and can make a safe decision.

The situation arose suddenly in the agency's public affairs office. Unlike the guide dog, the team didn't pause to examine the cognitive dissonance it was experiencing. The dog slowed down and assessed the situation. The public affairs staff rationalized it away and followed the unusual order. Splat!

Understanding the Real Risks

The human member of the human-guide dog team has a complex life. He has economic concerns, health concerns, social concerns, and more. The dog doesn't understand the sensitivity of client relations, of personnel evaluations from a regimented boss, or the tough economy in which losing a client or a job can undermine the security in one's life. These are real concerns.

The dog also has a real concern: the physical well-being of the person he is supporting. If the human is seriously injured or even killed, the risks the human is focused on will no longer be of concern. Without understanding all the complex aspects of that individual's life, the dog, nevertheless, chooses actions to avoid the most fundamental risks. What can we learn from this about Intelligent Disobedience?

Let's use the story of Betty Vinson.

If you're old enough, you may remember the story of her company, WorldCom, and its chief executive officer, Bernie Ebbers. You'd remember WorldCom because of the massive fraud—$3.8 billion—it committed, and Ebbers because he was sentenced to twenty-five years in jail. But you probably don't remember Betty Vinson. She worked about four levels below Mr. Ebbers as a senior manager in the accounting department, who at her peak made many times less salary than Mr. Ebbers and his executives. That didn't stop her from serving jail time.

Betty Vinson worked hard, was diligent, and grew with the company. She was loyal, often working late into the night to get her job done. She was a wife and a mom, cheered on her daughter at soccer games and volunteered in community service programs. She and her husband took pride in keeping their home and garden looking good. In other words, she was much like you or me or, if you're quite young, how you may be when you get a bit older and acquire some professional seniority and financial assets.

Then one day, Betty's direct supervisor asked her to step off the curb. Worldcom was having financial difficulty it did not want Wall Street to know about. So the supervisor's own superiors instructed him to move around money—a lot of money—more than three-quarters of a billion dollars—to mask the reality of the financial situation. He, in turn, instructed Betty Vinson to do the same.

At first she balked. The instruction violated accounting rules. That could cause trouble. She voiced her concern to her supervisor. He assured her that higher-ups knew the problem and wanted it done for the good of the company. They had assured him this was a one-time, never to be repeated action. Cognitive dissonance reared its head for both Betty and her supervisor. All the pieces that didn't make sense were swept aside by the sway of authority. The executives were smart people; surely, they wouldn't do something stupid! Betty Vinson stepped off the curb and made the adjustments to the accounting figures.

When the manipulated figures were about to be released publicly, Betty almost jumped back onto the curb—she considered resigning, even drafted a letter. But she didn't resign. After all, she had a very good job in a blue chip company that was just going through a difficult patch. Her salary was greater than her husband's. If she left WorldCom without another job, they faced financial risk to their lifestyle, their mortgage payments, their health care plans. Notice, this is now similar thinking to that of Ebbers and his cronies, though on a different scale. They, too, didn't want to risk the damage to the company's financial value or their own financial portfolios. So the team—executives and accountants—no longer had either partner focusing on the true risks, the mid- and long-term risks of their choices. They stepped off the curb in unison.

Once they did so, it was hard to get back onto the sidewalk. The underlying problems did not right themselves, and each subsequent financial quarter Betty Vinson was asked to cooperate "just one more time." The accounting violations to make the company appear financially sound became more flagrant. By the time six quarters of accounting manipulation had occurred, the evidence could not be concealed. One day the company internal auditor walked into Betty

Vinson's office and asked her to justify the accounting moves she had made. She could not do so. Neither could any of her superiors.

Betty turned witness for the federal government, which helped reduce her sentence but did not save her from serving time in jail. At the trial she told the court, "I felt like if I didn't make the entries I wouldn't be working here." True, that was the short-term risk. She also told the judge, "I certainly won't do anything like this again." True again, we hope, but there is no do-over. She saw the car coming and still stepped off the curb when her leaders said to do so. She paid the price for saying "yes" when she should have said "no."

Principles

In case you are thinking that these are pretty extreme examples, it is important to note that there are many instances of subordinates being pressured to do something to avoid short-term risk, while more serious long-term risks are ignored. And bear this in mind: when pressured to do something that violates legal, professional, or moral standards, it almost always feels like a sudden shock that can numb thinking and open us to cognitive dissonance.

What other kinds of examples have come to light in recent years? Here are just a few. Notice how wide are the range of activities:

Teachers pressured to give students answers to tests on which their school rank and funding will depend

Police pressured to underreport crime statistics when political figures need to demonstrate their effectiveness at reducing street violence

Football players urged to use concussion-causing "kill shots" on vulnerable opponents

Customs inspectors told to ignore incidents of pests on incoming plants to avoid triggering the requirement to fill out lengthy reports

Medical administrators told to file insurance claims that exaggerate the procedures used

Loan officers encouraged to declare nonexistent revenues so the borrowers would appear to qualify for mortgages they couldn't afford

Financial services clerks pressured to robo-sign home foreclosure notices without verifying the accuracy of the data

Grocery clerks told to repackage boxes of eggs that had reached their expiration date

Veterans Affairs hospital administrators falsifying patient wait times to obscure the backlog in providing critical services

Examples can occur in any profession. Perhaps they have in yours. When they do, you have to decide if you will step off the curb. Many, if not most, orders to do the wrong thing concern meeting numerical quotas or goals. Years ago, the guru of Quality Management, W. Edwards Deming, warned us of this pitfall. He argued against tying job performance ratings and monetary rewards to numerical goals. These exert pressure up and down the system to make the numbers look good, instead of continuously improving the work processes and systems to achieve true quality.

The case of WorldCom is simply a high-profile example of the excessive focus on making the numbers that is found in virtually every private and public sector organization. At this writing, the pressure to meet numerical performance goals is roiling the entire education profession. It is fine, even necessary to collect a certain amount of data on any system and its outputs in order to analyze where improvement is needed. It is generally deadly to overdo this and to tie awards and penalties, or even employment itself, to those metrics.

As attempts to improve education in the United States began focusing on the results of standardized tests to measure student, teacher, and school success, the pressure magnified at all levels to do the wrong thing. An alarming number of school administrators and teachers "stepped off the curb." News outlets across the country reported indictments, confessions, and trials of educators who succumbed to the pressure and found a multitude of unethical ways to raise test scores. When exposed, many offered the reason for altering test scores or finding other ways to manipulate them that we heard from Betty Vinson. They were afraid of losing their jobs. When exposed, many lost their jobs anyway or found themselves in courtrooms facing the legal consequences of fraud.

In the midst of these numerous instances of inappropriate obedience, a notable example of Intelligent Disobedience made headlines in Florida. More precisely, this was an example of Intelligent Disobedience walking up to the line of civil disobedience, per Florida law, with a willingness to step over that line if needed.

The teacher was Susan Bowles of Lawton Chiles Elementary School in Gainesville, Florida. Ms. Bowles had taught for twenty-six years and had an excellent record. As standardized testing requirements mounted, she found the volume and methodology of the tests being imposed on her K–2 students (yes, kindergarten through second grade) becoming grossly detrimental to her capacity, and that of her colleagues, to provide a quality education experience to those in her charge. After brainstorming with her colleagues about ways to comply with the requirement to administer these ongoing batteries of tests, she concluded it could not be done without fundamentally compromising her duty to educate her students appropriately at their level. She used social media to inform the parents of her students why she was choosing to disobey the orders to administer a particularly time-consuming and difficult to administer test—the Florida Assessment for Instruction in Reading, or FAIR. She acknowledged that doing so would probably cost her job, but her conscience called her to take a stand.

This story was picked up by other social media outlets and found its way into the mainstream media. Not all such cases have a happy ending. This case had a particularly satisfying one. In response to the outpouring of community and professional support for Ms. Bowles, and the attention brought by her to the adverse impact of the testing on the education environment, the Florida Commissioner of Education decided not to require FAIR testing for K–2 students.[1]

You who are reading this are almost certainly engaged in a system with short-term incentives based on numerical targets and metrics, either in your work life, your student life, or as a parent of a student in the educational system. These are situations in which you would do well to pay close attention to pressures exerted by short-term incentives. You may need to examine your own values and actions in relation to these incentives. What values are you willing to compromise to get a bonus, have your child get an outstanding report card, or for your school to get extra funding? It is easy for us to be outraged at others' behavior, but we, too, are susceptible to these pressures. Unless we are willing to confront ourselves on these matters, we are vulnerable to colluding with authorities who are also afraid of the penalties and tempted by the rewards tied to the metrics. Once we have confronted ourselves effectively and are ready to take a stand, we need to be mentally prepared to experience pressure from authorities who are also caught up in this system.

Some variation of the following steps is needed when faced with new or sudden instructions whose risks may not involve immediate consequences, but contain the potential for serious mid- or long-term consequences.

1. Let yourself register the surprised, somewhat stunned reaction you are feeling to being asked to do something wrong, something unethical or in poor judgment.

2. Resist the reflex to rationalize what you are being asked to do in order to resolve your discomfort; the discomfort is your ally in doing the right thing.

3. Slow down the action. Use language and body signals to do so: put up a hand like someone directing traffic and say, "Hold on a minute. . . ."

4. Give your higher functioning mental processes a chance to recover from the shock of the inappropriate order.

5. Examine what values are being violated and what are the real risks of complying, not just the short-term risk of not complying.

6. Ask tough, relevant questions about the orders you are receiving. Maybe you misinterpreted what you were being asked to do. Maybe you didn't. You have a right and an obligation to clarify the order.

7. Do not be assuaged by responses that are not answers, by attempts to rationalize the order, to shame you as being the only one questioning the order, or by promises of future correction of violations that are being ordered now.

8. Engage the authorities giving the order; help them see how it is not in their true interest to proceed in that direction; offer reasonable alternatives.

9. If you can't stop the leader from stepping off the curb into oncoming risk, refuse to join him or her in doing so. Understand the danger of saying "yes" when you should say "no."

10. Accept the short-term consequences of your choice. Appreciate the long-term consequences you most likely avoided.

CHAPTER SIX

The Dynamics of Authority and Obedience

"One must always question the relationship of obedience to a person's sense of the context in which he is operating."

STANLEY MILGRAM

W HAT IS GOING ON HERE? Why does there seem to be such prevalence of poor judgment in the face of orders from those in authority? Why is training needed to get people to do what common sense seems to require? Why are people obeying when they are uncomfortable doing so? Surely, you wouldn't obey in these types of situations!

Or would you?

Unfortunately, there is pretty hard evidence that about two-thirds of us would obey under certain circumstances even when we thought doing so was causing harm to others. This well-researched and documented evidence has been around for more than fifty years. It is so important that you would think it would be part of the professional training of anyone in a sensitive position, from mechanics who maintain vehicles that people trust with their lives to the intelligence services that must respect the law when conducting clandestine activities to protect their country. When I have been asked to speak to the intelligence community or armed forces, I have inquired about this because I did not want to spend time on material that was already well known in their culture. I found very few who were sufficiently familiar with this research and its application to their own situations.

I am going to review the research here because it is too important to not be part of the training of successive generations. I don't just mean professional training, I mean training as citizens of liberal democracies or, even more fundamentally, education as decent human beings. This is a call to those who design civics curricula to include this classic research and to design activities that connect it to the lives of successive waves of those who will occasionally need to intelligently disobey for the good of us all.

Dr. Stanley Milgram
and Obedience to Authority

First, let's set the historic stage for what have come to be known as the Milgram experiments conducted between 1960 and 1963.

This period is still psychologically the aftermath of the Second World War. I know this personally. When I was a boy growing up in Brooklyn, New York, I played a solitary ball game against the stone steps, or in the local vernacular "stoop," outside my row home. My personal variation of the game was to have each point I earned represent a Jew saved from the Nazi death camps. In my late teens, in 1964, I hitch-hiked through Serbia, then part of Yugoslavia. The first question I was always asked was "Are you German?" If I was, few would be willing to help me, even fifteen years after the German occupation of the country had ended. One fellow hitchhiker reported a German youth having been stoned by the townsfolk who had lived through the occupation. The larger Western world was still shocked by the reality that Germans, citizens of a highly advanced "civilized" country that brought the world brilliant music, literature, and art, could have obeyed a murderous regime and implemented orders to starve and kill millions of men, women, and children. Photographs of gaunt faces and skeletal bodies continue to haunt the collective psyche to this day, as they should.

From 1945 to 1948—well before 1960 when Milgram began his experiments— the victorious allied governments conducted the

Nuremberg trials of those accused of war crimes. The trials firmly established the principle that the claim of "just following orders" was not a defense against committing crimes. A series of principles were developed to guide the tribunals. The one germane to our discussion is Principle IV.

Nuremberg Principle IV states:

The fact that a person acted pursuant to an order of his Government or of a superior does not relieve him from responsibility under international law, provided a moral choice was in fact possible to him.

The trials were divided into two groups. The first and most famous was the trial of the Major War Criminals before the International Military Tribunal (IMT), which tried twenty-five of the most important captured leaders of the Third Reich. Many of these defendants received the death penalty or life in prison, though several received sentences of fifteen to twenty years and two were acquitted. The second group, informally known as the Subsequent Nuremberg trials is perhaps of greater interest for our purposes. There were twelve such trials including the doctors trial, the judges trial, the ministries trial, and the IG Farben trial and Krupp trial, the latter two being trials of industrialists. A minority of defendants were acquitted while many more received sentences ranging from one and half years to twenty years. (It is noteworthy that in this group only the doctors received death penalties in payment for the inhumane experimentation on helpless captives.) Regardless of their place in the hierarchy, the defense of "just following orders" did not absolve them of culpability.

Nor was the German example a unique aberration in twentieth-century history. Obedience to political programs for radically altering whole societies in Russia and China had resulted, or was resulting, in millions of additional deaths. Surely, the Western world had its own share of inhumane behavior, but cognitive dissonance and the sheer scale of the atrocities committed by "the other" (that which we consider to be "not us" and in relation to which we contrast our own identity) made those atrocities fixtures in postwar consciousness, like a nightmare whose images were hard to shake off.

Looming over this recent past was the potential mega-nightmare of the threat to the very existence of the human species through nuclear annihilation if orders to launch a nuclear attack were issued and obeyed. I once worked with a former officer in the Strategic Air Command who believed he had received orders to do just that and was halfway to the Soviet target when his crew was told to abort the mission. It was most likely a drill, if a terrifying one. Twenty years later, his craggy face and nervous eyes still showed signs of deep distress at the thought that he might have felt compelled to carry out that order if the situation had not been a drill and the order had not been withdrawn.

In this historic context, it seemed critical to understand more about obedience itself and, most urgently, obedience to destructive orders. Are people obedient solely out of fear for their own safety and lives if they disobey? Are they sadists who happily obey psychopathic leaders? Or are there other dynamics to obedience that, if understood, could serve as a way of altering the propensity of humans to obey when we should not? The Milgram experiments were surprisingly effective at answering these and related questions.

If you are already familiar with these experiments, you know that in the basic experiment, reproduced many times by Milgram and later by others, two out of every three subjects obeyed orders to repeatedly administer what they thought were painful and potentially lethal electric shocks to a victim.

"Well," you say, "that's horrible! I know I would be the one out of three who didn't do that!"

Everyone reading about the experiments likes to think this. Of course, it can't be true for everyone, can it? In fact, Milgram showed how erroneous our view on this is in a clever ancillary experiment.

He gave briefings on the experiment to 110 individuals from three profiles: students, psychiatrists, and middle-class adults of varying professions. More than 75 percent predicted they personally would stop by 150 volts (strong shock) and *none* predicted they would administer beyond 300 volts. This was far short of the potentially lethal 450 volts for which the experiment seemed to call and which many obeyed the command to administer. Clearly, how we like to see ourselves is not in itself predictive of how we would actually behave in the face of destructive orders.

So let's examine what it is about the experiment that caused people of decent intentions and free will to fail to intelligently disobey. I have found that even those with prior familiarity with the experiments rarely have done more than scratch the surface of what they reveal. Remember our central question: *after being taught to obey authority our whole lives, what does it really take to disobey?*

The Experiment

Dr. Milgram's laboratory was in New Haven, Connecticut, at Yale University. Although it is easiest to use students as subjects, he chose to reach into the broader community to ensure he was recruiting individuals from a range of ages, backgrounds, and social classes. At a certain point in the experiments, he moved the site from the campus buildings to a somewhat rundown office building in the neighboring city of Bridgeport to eliminate any effect the distinguished university itself was having on subjects. He did his best within the social lens of the era to ensure the data would be representative of a range of humanity. Although he primarily used men in his experiments, he did at least one full experiment with only women as the subjects and found the results to be nearly identical to that of men. His experiments were replicated by others with remarkable consistency in different countries, giving support for generalizing his findings at least in Western cultures. Because of the nature of the experiment itself, which I will explain next, it is no longer considered ethical to perform the experiment exactly as Milgram did due to the extreme stress subjects often experienced.

There was a simple structure to the experiment. After establishing a baseline of response to this structure, Dr. Milgram carefully introduced variables that give us a lot of information on *what helps people disobey* destructive orders. In my view, this is the aspect of the experiments that may be the most important, though it has been given less attention. Let's start with examining the basic experiment.

There are three essential figures in the experiment:

The first is "the experimenter." This is not Milgram but an individual hired to play the role. In the original experiments, this role was performed by a thirty-one-year-old biology teacher whose appearance Milgram describes as "somewhat stern." He was dressed in a gray technician's coat. This is important information because the laboratory coat is his symbol of authority.

The second is "the victim." He plays the role of "a learner" who receives electric shocks when he answers questions incorrectly. The victim did not actually receive shocks but was trained to display increasing signs of emotional and physical distress as the experiment progressed. By all accounts, his acting was completely convincing. This role in the original experiments was played by someone whom Milgram describes as a "mild-mannered and likeable" forty-seven-year-old Irish American man. (To eliminate the effect of personality on the results, at a later point Milgram used a second team in which "the experimenter" and "the victim" had generally opposite personalities to the first team, with no material results on the outcome.)

The third is the real subject of the experiment, though he doesn't know that. He is told that he is "the teacher," so Milgram calls him "the naïve subject." He is misled to believe that the learner ("the victim") is the subject. In each variation of the experiment, Milgram used forty different adults as naïve subjects.

How did the experiment work? The teacher (the naïve subject) is given a learning task to administer to the learner (the victim).

The teacher is sat in front of what he is told is a shock generator. It does not actually generate shocks, but he doesn't know that. The shock generator has thirty levers labeled from 15 volts to 450 volts in 15-volt increments. Each group of four levers is clearly marked from "slight shock" at the low end, through successive labels until at the higher ends they are marked as "intense shock," "extreme intensity shock," "danger: severe shock." The final two levers are simply marked "XXX."

Each time the learner gives an incorrect answer to the prepared questions posed by the teacher, the teacher must administer a shock, always one level above the previous shock. In order to make the act appear real, the teacher (naïve subject) is given a sample shock from the 45-volt lever. This is the only lever that actually generates a shock, and it gives just strong enough of a jolt to convince the naïve subject that the generator is real.

Now let's stop for a moment and ask why would anyone agree to perform the role of the teacher once they believed they understood what the experiment entailed? Milgram had thought about this. He wrote:

> A pretext had to be devised that would justify the administration of electric shock by the naïve subject. This is true because in every instance of legitimate authority the subordinate must perceive some connection, however tenuous, between the specific type of authority and the commands he issues.[1]

Milgram is making an important point. Think back to WorldCom or to the emergency room physician. Orders were coming not just from any authority, but from individuals who were perceived to have legitimate authority in those situations. For that matter, think back to our guide dog. It doesn't take orders from just any human. It comfortably ignores orders from anyone other than its human handler. But when the legitimate authority issues an order that could be unsafe to implement, a decision must be made of whether to obey. This is almost a paradox: *the danger that we will obey orders we should not obey almost always comes from what we perceive to be legitimate authority.*

In Milgram's experiment, he created this legitimacy by having the experimenter carefully explain that the purpose of the activity was to test one of the prevalent learning theories: that punishing mistakes can increase learning. They were researching to find if this were true and, if so, what level of punishment was most effective. This was enough of a reason to give an experimenter, dressed in a lab coat, legitimacy to order administering electric shocks.

Once legitimacy was established, the naïve subject watched the learner being strapped to a chair in an adjacent room with electrodes attached to his wrist. The naïve subject (the teacher) began asking questions through a two-way sound system. As the learner gave wrong answers, the teacher was to administer an increased level of shock. The learner (the victim) was trained to make certain sounds of discomfort and protest at each new level:

75–105 volts	Grunts
120 volts	Shouts that the shocks were becoming painful
135 volts	Painful groans
150 volts	"Experimenter! Get me out of here! I refuse to go on!"
180 volts	"I can't stand the pain!" (from here on, insisting he be let out)
270 volts	An agonized scream
300 volts	Shouts in desperation, "I won't give any more answers to the test!"

(At this point the experimenter instructs the teacher to treat a "no answer" as a wrong answer and to administer the next level of shock.)

315 volts and up	Agonized screams, no answers to questions
330 to 450 volts	No further sounds or answers

How were the teacher and the experimenter responding to this highly disturbing situation?

The good news is that most teachers expressed discomfort with the process as the learner became more agitated. They often indicated they didn't wish to continue. Why is this important? Because it clearly shows that this cross-sampling of humans were not enjoying inflicting harm on another human being. It was not sadistic delight at inflicting pain that was contributing to their actions. In fact, many became very disturbed by the situation. So why did two-thirds continue despite their discomfort at doing so?

The experimenter was provided with a series of responses, or "prods," that he was required to give to the hesitations and protests at continuing. If one didn't work, he would use the next in the sequence. They were:

Prod 1:   *Please continue,* or, *Please go on.*

Prod 2:   *The experiment requires that you continue.*

Prod 3:   *It is absolutely essential that you continue*

Prod 4:   *You have no other choice, you* must *go on.*

These were spoken firmly, but not harshly. If necessary, the experimenter could reassure the teacher by saying,

"Although the shocks may be painful, there is no permanent tissue damage, so please go on."

If the teacher protested that the learner did not want to go on, the experimenter said,

"Whether the learner likes it or not, you must go on until he has learned all the word pairs correctly. So please go on."

Note, this is *all* the experimenter is allowed to say. There are no coercive threats. It is not fear of personal harm or loss of the meager fee that was given to each volunteer that is driving the subject to overcome his discomfort with obeying. That is an important factor to rule out in this situation. So what is it that is creating obedience when the subject is trying to be released from obeying?

We are left to conclude that it is the relationship to what is perceived as legitimate authority, even though what that authority is requiring is highly problematic. This is a central fact to absorb: the mere appearance of legitimate authority often outweighs an individual's own assessment of the situation and his or her sense of right and wrong.

To appreciate this more fully, I am going to ask you to do an uncomfortable mental exercise with me. Visualize yourself in the following situation.

You are an upstanding American soldier. You have been trained to the highest levels of professionalism. In addition to your specialty, you have been trained in the rules of warfare and on codes of conduct in warfare such as the Geneva Convention. You have been deployed to Iraq during what came to be known as the second Gulf War. It is a hot, hostile environment. Everyone is there to do a job.

You are assigned to an interrogation team. You feel the full weight of responsibility to extract information from captured individuals who appear to have been combatants. The information could reveal and disrupt future plans of terrorism or military attack. You and your team are using the range of interrogation techniques in which you have been trained. They are not producing as much information as senior command believes they should.

A new intelligence specialist is brought in and given command of your team. He explains that due to the urgency in the situation, he is authorized to use a technique known as waterboarding. You know about this technique because it is used in small doses to train our own soldiers to survive should they be captured and tortured in violation of the Geneva Convention, but you have never seen it in use as an interrogation technique.

Later that week a "high-value" prisoner is brought in. He has not responded to other forms of interrogation. He is taken to a small, secure room and bound hand and foot on a board laid across the floor. A wet cloth is placed over his mouth and nose. You are told to start pouring water from a can onto the cloth. The prisoner immediately gags and starts violently trying to break free of his restraints. You hesitate and are told to "go on."

You continue pouring water for twenty seconds while the prisoner writhes. You are told to stop. The cloth is removed and the prisoner is allowed to take three or four gasping breaths before his mouth and nose are again covered. You are ordered to resume pouring. The prisoner again gags, his eyes bulge, and his whole body convulses. The board he is strapped to is shaking and smacking against the concrete. You hesitate again, repulsed by what you are seeing and by the fleeting thought that this is the illegal torture you were trained to survive.

"Go on, we need to do this." You are told and reluctantly comply. This is a superior officer, trained in intelligence gathering, who is issuing the command. You are told to continue for thirty seconds this time. The prisoner is frantic. He is experiencing drowning. You feel sickened by what you are doing. You suggest that maybe that's enough. The officer tells you that we need to continue. This time you are instructed to pour for forty seconds. When the cloth is removed the prisoner looks half-dead.

Even just reading this account, can you feel the pressure that orders from someone who appears to be a legitimate authority serving a legitimate need exerts on the choice you make? Can you sense how extremely difficult it would be to refuse to obey despite your discomfort?

Of course, the scenario wasn't hypothetical, other than imagining your own involvement. This is what actually occurred in recent years. The "high-value detainee" was subjected to this for many subsequent days if he did not or could not reveal information that those in command considered he may be withholding. Waterboarding has since been deemed to be torture by the US government and has officially ceased to be an allowable technique. But fine, upstanding American soldiers were complicit in its use when instructed by authority to employ it.

Yet, not everyone obeyed orders. A retired officer confided in me that a buddy of his had been at Abu Ghraib prison in Iraq and had been instructed to use waterboarding. His friend pointed out to the intelligence officer issuing the order that he thought waterboarding violated the Geneva Convention. He was told to do as he was ordered. His friend had the presence of mind to say,

"I will need that order in writing before executing it."

That was the last he heard of the matter. No one was willing to put the order in writing. That removed the legitimacy of the authority figures. It is an important response to bear in mind if you ever find yourself in an analogous situation.

What else can we learn from Milgram's experiments that would help us understand the mechanisms of the tendency to obey when we should not? And what can we learn about the factors that help us resist the pressure to obey, if that would be the right thing to do?

Defiance: The New England Minister

Milgram shares anecdotal material as well as statistical observations. Let's look at the experience of a man who teaches at a divinity school. Milgram reports this exchange in response to the experimenter's "prods."[2]

Experimenter: *It's absolutely essential to the experiment that we continue.*

Subject: *I understand the statement, but I don't understand why the experiment is placed above this person's life.*

Experimenter: *There is no permanent tissue damage.*

Subject:	*Well, that's your opinion. If he doesn't want to continue, I'm taking orders from him.*
Experimenter:	*You have no other choice, sir, you must go on.*
Subject:	*If this were Russia, maybe, but not in America.*

We can admire the subject's pluck, but how are we to understand it? We need to put the last statement in the cold war era context to fully appreciate it. America was considered the land of the free, pitted in an existential battle against the Soviet system that placed little value on individual human rights. The subject invoked his cultural heritage as more fundamental and, therefore, more legitimate than the experimenter. Milgram observes that the subject is not intimidated by the experimenter's status, and in fact views him as *"a dull technician who does not see the full implications of what he is doing."*

This is a powerful observation and, moving beyond a cold war mentality, very important to our contemporary technical society. Our lives are full of encounters with technicians who order us to stand behind certain lines, walk through X-rays, sign documents, provide personal data, and the like. In a damning episode of the TV show *Candid Camera*,[3] the producers set up a phony X-ray scanner at an airport security line and told passengers they needed to lie down on the conveyer to be sent through the X-ray machine, assuring them it was safe. Incredibly, eleven out of twelve complied! One by one, they lay down on the conveyer belt, folded their arms across their chest, and were sent through the pseudo-machine! In America, not Russia! This would be very funny, as *Candid Camera* stunts usually are, if the implications weren't so frightening. How conditioned have we become to obeying technical authority, whatever color its lab coat or uniform? Where would we draw the line at obedience?

Elsewhere, Milgram observes that once we abrogate our own responsibility for following an order, we focus on implementing the order with technical proficiency. I have experienced this firsthand as airport security procedures steadily increased after the attacks of

September 11, 2001, on US landmarks that used hijacked commercial airplanes. Although understanding the need for increased security, I internally railed against the process that seemed to be making us into compliant sheep. Yet, as time went on, I found myself focusing less on the problematic dynamics and more on executing the procedures efficiently. The security screening technology in that period required passengers to take certain actions before passing through the equipment. I became aware that I experienced a certain amount of pride in how rapidly I unlaced my shoes, whipped my computer out of its case, slid off my belt, grabbed my clear plastic quart bag of toiletries out of the roll-a-board pocket, stuffed everything into trays on the conveyor belt at a speed suited to a relay race, took every last tissue out of my pockets, and assumed the arms over head posture before needing to be told to do so in the full body scanner in airports that use those. *Candid Camera* could have a good laugh at my expense!

Maybe you have experienced something similar—a touch of pride at how good you became at the airport screening procedure? A touch of scorn and impatience at those who fumble and do it wrong? Let me note, that sense of pride I experience is not only laughable, it is highly dangerous! Adolf Eichmann, one of the key architects of the mass extermination of Jews in Nazi death camps in World War II, also experienced pride in his technical proficiency. That is what occurs when we allow technical requirements to substitute for our own determination of what is appropriate action.

A first step to interrupting this dangerous progression might be to learn from the minister Milgram quotes. He questioned the legitimacy of the source of the orders, regardless of the gray lab coat uniform. It appears that it would help us to exercise Intelligent Disobedience if we train ourselves to mentally differentiate the orders we receive almost routinely from technicians who are following a script and those coming from knowledgeable authority who hold themselves responsible for outcomes. That mental differentiation is at least a start in the right direction. This is the second step in the three-step sequence we examined earlier about which orders should be obeyed:

Is the authority legitimate and reasonably competent?

Then we can make choices about the order itself.

After the minister breaks off the experiment, the subject is debriefed, as all the subjects were. The true purpose of the experiment is explained and he is asked,

"What in your opinion is the most effective way of strengthening resistance to inhumane authority?"

I have rarely heard a more important question if we are to reduce inflicting undeserved harm on others, as occurs in too many contexts throughout our world. The subject replies,

"If one has as one's ultimate authority God, then it trivializes human authority."

Milgram makes a cogent observation here: this individual's capacity to resist did not come from *"the repudiation of authority but in the substitution of good—that is, divine—authority for bad."*[4] Milgram is not making a religious point here. He is observing that to resist destructive obedience we need to hold a stronger obedience to something else—to a value, a principle, an oath, a belief system.

In the next chapter we are going to examine variations of the basic experiment that point us toward ways we can alter the social context to reduce the incidence of inappropriate obedience. Before we do, though, we might ask: Are these experiments, conducted more than fifty years ago, worthy of the attention we are giving them?

Is Milgram Still Relevant?— The Game of Death

In 2010, fifty years after Milgram's first experiments, a French documentary maker conceived the idea to replicate Milgram's basic experiment in the context of a TV show pilot. As in the original experiment, the learner was not actually receiving shocks, but his screams were realistic and anguished. The teacher believed the shocks were real—all the way to 450 volts. Apparently, the documentarian either did not know or did not fall under the injunction to researchers against repeating this experiment due to the ethical concerns of placing the subjects under excessive stress. His motive was to demonstrate the power of authority, compounded by the power of TV and a thrill-seeking audience, to goad ordinary people into doing extraordinarily harmful acts. The following are excerpts from a BBC report of the event:

Row over "Torture" on French TV

By David Chazan, BBC News, Paris

A disturbing French TV documentary has tried to demonstrate how well-meaning people can be manipulated into becoming torturers or even executioners.

The hugely controversial *Game of Death* was broadcast in prime-time on a major terrestrial channel, France 2, on Wednesday.

It showed 80 people taking part in what they thought was a game show pilot.

As it was only a trial, they were told they wouldn't win anything, but they were given a nominal 40 euro fee.

Before the show, they signed contracts agreeing to inflict electric shocks on other contestants.

One by one, they were put in a studio resembling the sets of popular game shows.

They were then asked to zap a man they believed was another contestant whenever he failed to answer a question correctly—with increasingly powerful shocks of up to 460 volts.

Blind Obedience

Egged on by a glamorous presenter, cries of "punishment" from a studio audience, and dramatic music, the overwhelming majority of the participants obeyed orders to continue delivering the shocks—despite the man's screams of agony and pleas for them to stop.

Eventually, he fell silent, presumably because he had died or lost consciousness.

The contestants didn't know that the man, strapped in a chair inside a cubicle so they couldn't see him, was really an actor. There were no shocks and it was all an experiment to see how far they would go.

Only 16 of the 80 participants stopped before the ultimate, potentially lethal shock.

"No one expected this result," intoned a commentary. "Eighty per cent of the candidates went to the very end."

The show was billed as a warning against blindly obeying authority—and a critique of reality TV shows in which participants are humiliated or hurt.

Some of the participants smiled or laughed nervously as they delivered the shocks, although most were obviously stressed and troubled by the action.

Many said they wanted to stop but were convinced by the presenter to continue.

The show was inspired by an experiment at Yale University in the 1960s by social psychologist Stanley Milgram.

He used similar methods to investigate how people could come to take part in mass murder.

Jean-Leon Beauvois, a psychologist who took part in the documentary, says he and other members of the team spent months analysing the results.

"When they signed the contract, participants were placed in the position of executioners," he said.

"These were people like others, not exceptional, but 80% of them let themselves be drawn into becoming torturers."[5]

If you watch video of this TV experiment, you will see a multiracial, young, well-dressed audience vehemently urging on the teacher to administer shocks. The few who resisted came from a range of backgrounds. Some backgrounds, such as previous experience with brutal dictatorships, explained their capacity to resist. Others who also had backgrounds that should have equipped them to resist did not. The individual profile of successful resisters remains elusive, if one even exists. Rather than focus on backgrounds that can't in any case be changed, it seems we need to focus on changing the context so that all potential actors have a repertory of productive responses to unconscionable orders.

In the video of the staged game show, we see an African woman resisting shocking the learner. She is troubled by what she is doing. She is egged on by the game show host and the audience. The woman obeys up to a point and then will go no further. She is led off stage in great distress at what she has already done. Yet, she is among the mere 20 percent who do break off the "game." So we see that human behavior in the Milgram experiments is not an artifact of another, less enlightened age. It is our age, or possibly every age. What will we do about it?

Fortunately, Milgram did variations of this experiment that help us answer that question. We will examine those in the following chapter. Let's first summarize the disturbing picture painted by the basic experiment:

1. Most of us believe we would not follow harmful orders.

2. The Milgram obedience experiments taught us we cannot rely on the belief that we would not follow harmful orders.

3. Most people will follow harmful orders, even if they find them disturbing.

4. The experimental data are supported by numerous examples of inappropriate obedience in life.

5. We confuse technical agents, who are themselves "just following orders," with legitimate authority that is knowledgeable, accountable, and has the power to modify or cancel orders that are causing harm.

6. We can derive satisfaction from using speed and accuracy to comply with technical orders, thereby occluding the immorality of following the orders.

7. There is a tendency to focus on the authority in front of us, whether technical or legitimate, rather than focus on that which we consider to be a "higher authority" from where we derive our moral bearings.

Let's see what Milgram found to help us change these widespread and very problematic tendencies.

CHAPTER SEVEN

Changing the Dynamics

"When an individual wishes to stand in opposition
to authority, he does best to find support for
his position from others in his group."[1]

STANLEY MILGRAM

I N HIS BOOK *Obedience to Authority*, Milgram notes:

The crux of the study is to vary the factors believed to alter the degree
of obedience to the experimental commands and to learn under what
conditions submission to authority is most probable and under what
conditions defiance is brought to the fore.[2]

In the many years I have talked about the Milgram experiments
with those professionals and managers who were familiar with them,
I have never heard this emphasis. Milgram scholars know about the
variations, but there has been a failure to effectively disseminate
this knowledge broadly in the culture. We seem to be so stunned by
the indictment of human behavior revealed by the core experiment
(though Milgram was careful not to make moral judgments) that we
have missed the potential gold to be found in the dark soil he mined.
What helps individuals intelligently disobey?

Let's examine a few of the variations Milgram did on the basic
experiment to see what else we can learn about obedience or defiance
in the face of questionable, dangerous, or outright inhumane orders.

Closeness of Subject

Milgram tested several degrees of closeness of the subject to the learner (victim). When the learner was remote, in another room, 65 percent of the teachers complied all the way to 450 volts when they could only hear voice feedback from the anguished learner. When the learner was placed in the same room as the subject, and his physical anguish could be seen as well as heard, full compliance dropped to 40 percent. When the experiment was altered so the subject had to force the learner's hand into full contact with the shock plate, only 30 percent (less than half the original number) complied all the way to 450 volts. There are some sobering reflections we can make based on this data.

We live in an age of drone warfare and cyberattacks that can remotely assassinate targeted individuals and groups and disable whole cities' power and water supplies. The individual who "pulls the lever" creates this effect without any direct experience of the devastation caused by these acts. Based on this variation of Milgram's experiment, the conditions are near-perfect for compliance to authority. Is this acceptable to us? Is it our ideal to create human drones to launch mechanical drones? If not, how will we instill ethical responsibility in those charged with remotely executing these orders? What degree of information is required to enable them to make ethical choices regarding that execution? What feedback loops on the impact of their actions are appropriate in helping them determine whether to continue the action?

At the other end of the spectrum, we must contemplate that a significant minority of subjects (30 percent) will still execute harmful orders even if it means forcefully and physically holding the victim down in order to do so. Does this mean that there will always be some who can be relied on as henchmen of power run amok? Are there any social mechanisms to counteract this dark tendency? Will we find some counter measures in further variations of the experiment?

Closeness of Authority

Milgram postulated that if distance from the victim was a variable, so could distance from the authority affect compliance. He set up a variation in which the researcher, after giving initial instructions, left the laboratory and continued to give orders by telephone. Full compliance dropped to just 20 percent! Some of the subjects began to covertly disobey by administering only low-level shocks while falsely reporting that they were increasing the shock level as required. These instances were a different form of Intelligent Disobedience in which there is no overt resistance to authority but the subject nevertheless does what he deems is the right thing.

All Intelligent Disobedience is contextual—requiring evaluation of the degree of consequences of obeying and of disobeying, both to others and to self, and making a choice based on this evaluation as to what to do and how to do it. It could be deduced from this variation of the experiment that the more the physical presence of authority is required in order to exact compliance to potentially harmful orders, the less truly legitimate is that authority. Perhaps this is another criterion individuals can use or be trained to use in order to evaluate the context of a situation and whether it is appropriate to obey. Let's return for a moment to the waterboarding scene to see how this might work.

Imagine again that you are part of a detail of enlisted soldiers who have been instructed to waterboard a high-value prisoner. After a couple of rounds of waterboarding have been completed, the senior officer leaves the area and tells you to continue while he is gone. Instead you and the group find yourselves hesitating, maybe only pouring water for ten seconds and leaving more space between doses for the prisoner to recover his breath and reduce his panic.

When the senior officer returns you resume the full treatment, placing accountability on the officer. You notice that you are behaving differently in the presence of this authority from how you are behaving in his absence. This should trigger an individual and group examination of the morality of the command. The evasion of the order is an indicator that the locus of accountability needs to shift back to you—a central aspect of Intelligent Disobedience—whether or not the senior officer returns to the scene. Is the order legitimate? Is it producing beneficial or harmful consequences? If called before an investigation of the matter, would you find yourself claiming you were just following orders? This is a bright red danger signal! If this signal appears, it should be a cue to find a way of creating the physical or mental distance needed from the authority figure to work out what is the right thing, and then do that—whether it is intelligent obedience or Intelligent Disobedience.

The essence, in either case, is what you DO. It is *not* what you *feel* or what you say. It is the choice you make and what you actually DO.

Milgram offers the example of a subject who expresses repeated objections to the experiment but continues to administer the increasingly strong shocks. He observes there is a disassociation between the subject's words and actions. There is also an out-of-place politeness toward the experimenter. Milgram notes, "He thinks he is killing someone, yet he uses the language of the tea table."[3] We may think we can let ourselves off the moral hook by saying "I didn't feel what we were doing was right. I told them we should stop." No, this doesn't absolve us to the world and shouldn't absolve us to ourselves. We still obeyed. We were polite. We followed orders we should not have followed. It is always our actions for which we will be held accountable.

Conflicting Authorities

There is a standard in many cultures that two parents ought not to disagree in front of their children. By extension, in many groups it is considered bad form for two authority figures to disagree in front of subordinates. It is true that such disagreement may generate discomfort on the part of those who witness it and uncertainty as to who is in charge and whose lead to follow. Is this always a bad thing?

Milgram structured one variation on the experiment by introducing two researchers, both in lab coats. They took turns giving instructions. While they were in agreement, this posed no problem. When the experiment reached the 150 volt level, which is the level when the victim first protests vehemently, one of the researchers says the experiment needs to be stopped. The other expresses the usual response: "The experiment requires that we go on." They each repeat their contrary position several times. In this variation, *not a single subject followed the orders to continue.*

There is obviously an important lesson in this data. Life is often not so simple that there is only one authority figure. Often there are multiple authority figures, whether at our airport screening, the hospital emergency room, the WorldCom accounting department, or the school where you work or study. We are discovering in this data that obedience occurs within a social context. It is not just the individual receiving and acting on the order who is culpable (though he is), or even just the individual giving the harmful order (though he is). The rest of the system is also responsible. We will get to the role of other nonauthority participants shortly. First, let's examine the role of third-party authority figures in the dynamic.

We see from Milgram's data that one authority figure countermanding another is sufficient to completely disrupt compliance to the harmful order. The second authority figure did not hold rank above the other. He simply held equal legitimacy by reason of his role and its symbols. His taking a moral stand vis-à-vis the researcher who insisted on continuing the experiment was almost completely effective in reducing obedience to harmful orders. It seems that this places *even greater responsibility* on peers of authority figures to stop destructive acts than on the recipients of the orders. Yet, social dynamics make it no easier for peers of authority to do this than for subordinates. The same ability to step back and rise above the pressures of the moment are needed for peers to act.

Let me share a recent story of a young friend to illustrate this, a new school teacher, highly committed to teaching and her students' welfare. I will call her Marcy. Marcy had a colleague who taught another class at the same level. I will call her Michelle.

Michelle had a somewhat difficult personality and relations had been strained between her and Marcy. One day Marcy needed to borrow something from the other classroom. When she walked in, she found a student duct-taped to a chair! He was immobilized in the chair in plain sight of Michelle and the class. Obviously, Michelle had either done the duct-taping, or ordered it or, even less plausibly, condoned it being done by other students. Marcy was reflexively shocked but stifled her natural response out of concern for worsening her already delicate relationship with Michelle. Seeing Marcy, Michelle asked if she would watch the class for five minutes while she changed clothes for the next activity. Marcy agreed. When Michelle left, Marcy asked the student who was bound to the chair if he was okay? He seemed to indicate that he was, so Marcy did nothing further.

The next day, the parents of the student came to the school principal outraged at what had been done to their son. The principal confirmed their story with Michelle who had indeed taken the action as a disciplinary measure. The principal immediately dismissed her from her employment for grossly unacceptable behavior. The following day, Marcy came to work as usual. Through further investigation, the principal had discovered that Marcy had also been in the classroom for a few minutes and had done nothing to counter Michelle's actions. She, too, was dismissed on the spot.

We may be inclined to discount this as an outrageous example that isn't reflective of the everyday world in which we live and work. I thought so, until I read a report written for the US Senate, Health,

Education, Labor and Pensions committee titled the *Dangerous Use of Seclusion and Restraint Remains Widespread and Difficult to Remedy*, February 12, 2014. The report starts with the provocative sentence:

> *"This past August an Arizona teacher used duct tape to restrain a second grader to a chair because she was getting up to sharpen her pencil too frequently."*

The executive summary of the report cites at least 66,000 incidents of seclusion or restraint used in the first year of reporting in 2009–2010. Other sources cite the incidence of these practices as high as a quarter of a million in subsequent years! Federal law on the use of restraints and seclusion did not cover school instances of this, and the use of these practices varied among school systems. Thus it fell to the discretion of the local authority figures until recently, when the practice was banned in all but extreme circumstances such as when there is a need to prevent physical harm to the student or others.

Marcy is a very dedicated teacher and, happily, was able to have the mark expunged from her record. She is entering a new school system, having learned a very important lesson. Her silence in an attempt to avoid adverse social consequences for speaking up made her complicit in the act of her colleague. The principal's reaction may seem unfair since it treated Marcy with the same level of culpability as the teacher who had actually bound the student to the chair and kept him there for the whole period. Perhaps the reaction was harsher than needed, yet it correctly sent a message of the accountability of all authority figures who become aware of harmful behavior to act to interrupt the behavior, not just leave doing so to those in the chain of command.

Marcy could have asked Michelle to step outside for a moment and confronted her in the hallway out of earshot of her students. Avoiding publicly embarrassing the other authority figure, if possible, is a good relationship principle. If that were insufficient to dissuade Michelle to cease the behavior, speaking up publicly may have been the course required to disrupt the harmful behavior, despite the social discomfort that would create.

The Power of the Bystander

There is a vast amount of literature these days on bullying in schools, in virtual electronic spaces, and in the workplace. The preponderance of the literature focuses on not tolerating bullies and on better supporting their victims and equipping them to withstand bullying behavior. Only a few authors give the attention due to the third actor in the bullying dynamic—the bystander, though fortunately this seems to be changing. The bystander is present in the vicinity of the bullying but is not the direct target of the traumatizing behavior. Therefore, the bystander is better equipped psychologically to respond to the situation. These authors correctly identify the bystander as the actor with the greatest potential power to interrupt the destructive behavior.[4]

One of these authors, Barbara Coloroso, correctly observes that where state power turns genocidal, whether in Nazi Germany or any of the other dismal instances of genocide, the same structure applies. It is the silence of the majority who are bystanders that permits the crime to occur.

Although workplace bullies may be positional authority figures, many are not; school yard and virtual bullies are certainly not. Nevertheless, through their campaigns of terror, they develop a pseudo-legitimacy that makes others comply with their instructions to participate in the bullying. This has become a serious concern for school administrators, teachers, and parents in the education and online social systems and for human resource directors in the workplace. What can be done to break the power of the bully-authority?

Milgram devised a variation of his experiment that shows us a path for colleagues or bystanders to trigger Intelligent Disobedience. Later research on bullying itself corroborates the principles that surfaced in this variation.

Milgram placed the "naïve" subject between two other individuals who appear to be fellow teachers in the experiment. In fact, they are "confederates" who have been given exact roles to play. Teacher 1 (confederate 1) is assigned the task of reading the paired words to the learner. Teacher 2 (confederate 2) reports whether the learner's answers are correct. Teacher 3 (the naïve subject) pulls the levers to administer shocks.

At 150 volts, teacher 1 refuses to go on, gets up from the table, and seats himself elsewhere in the room despite the experimenter's demands that the experiment requires continuing. The naïve subject is told to take over the role of reading the questions while continuing the role of administering shocks. By 195 volts, 32 percent of the participants refused to continue. At 210 volts, the second confederate, teacher 2, also refuses. He relocates himself to another seat, saying he is willing to answer the experimenter's questions afterward but not to further participate in the experiment. An additional 30 percent of subjects immediately also refuse to continue. Only 10 percent continue to the end of the experiment at 450 volts. Ninety percent have resisted the urgings of authority to complete the experiment!

Milgram considers the lessons learned from this variation of the experiment as the most effective at reducing obedience to an authority that is issuing harmful orders. He identifies three principal reasons:

1. Most of us have internalized standards of behavior; when one or more others resist orders that violate those standards, it normalizes resistance to the orders.

2. If we see others take a stand without being unduly penalized by authority, we recalculate the risks involved of doing so ourselves.

3. If others refuse to participate in the harmful acts, we become aware that if we continue to comply, the group's sanctions may turn on us.

Some of this is obviously problematic. What if authority does penalize individuals who first disobey? That is a tactic often applied by those seeking to hold onto power through force. That is precisely why the most important act of disobedience is often that of the second or third resister. Their support for the first resister tips the calculations of others. Instead of placing greater weight on the power of formal authority or pseudo-authority, others begin placing greater weight on the power of social norms, of doing what we intuitively know is the right thing. The authority loses standing and his orders lose force.

We are assuming, of course, that the social norms that replace the force of authority uphold human values of decency; if they don't, and the history of groups repressing other groups tells us they may not, Intelligent Disobedience will need to find its own path, independent of either authority or convention. The internal compass pointing us to the right thing to do will need to be our primary orientation. How to give it greater weight than the social pressures around us will not come easily for many. We will examine the preparation needed to do so in succeeding chapters.

One Final Variation

There are other variations of the basic experiment that hold lessons on obedience and disobedience with which researchers and teachers of Milgram's works are familiar. For our purposes, I want to shine a light on one more variation of the basic experiment, the one that is the most frightening. Why? Because in this variation, 90 percent of the subjects comply with the experiment to the end! It is also frightening because it is the experiment that tells us why most individuals in large bureaucracies participate in destructive acts when they do: they themselves are not directly and immediately causing harm.

In this variation of the experiment, the subject does not administer shocks to the victim. The subject is given one of the ancillary roles like reading the question or documenting the answers. Because the subject is not directly causing pain, there is less psychological strain. The norms of the experiment itself prevail over greater moral norms. The experiment norms include the agreement to participate, the perception of legitimate authority and legitimate purpose, the social evidence of peer participation, and the absence of personal culpability in administering the pain.

Transfer this from the experiment to the case examples we have seen. This is not the soldier pouring water onto the wet towel over the prisoner's nose and mouth as he gasps violently for air. This is the analyst who identifies the prisoner as a possible high-value target for enhanced questioning. The analyst is doing her job, fulfilling her duty, implementing her training. She does not have to grapple with the immediate consequences of her analysis and the recommendations that proceed from it.

In the complex society in which we live, most of us occupy the equivalent of the analyst's role. We are not knowingly installing life-threatening equipment in automobiles—we work in a contracting office using accepted standards to purchase ignition parts at the lowest cost. We are not administering ineffective medicine to a dangerously sick patient—we are part of a research team cleaning up messy statistical data in a drug trial so efficacy can be more readily evaluated. We are not intentionally contributing to increased juvenile diabetes—we are providing affordable school lunches that can be predictably delivered to the cafeteria and appeal to the students' taste. We are not advocating inhumane factory working conditions on the other side of the globe—we are upgrading our phones to the newest user-friendly technology.

In these cases and a thousand like them, we are not directly harming a fellow human being. We are not hearing or seeing suffering caused earlier or later in the chain of events. We can screen out the problematic information on the periphery of our awareness and focus on doing the jobs to which we are assigned.

My analysis of this example slips from the narrower domain of Intelligent Disobedience to a direct order, into the more difficult domain of principled refusal to participate in a system producing harm. This is a hybrid somewhere between Intelligent Disobedience and civil disobedience. It is a standard that can be very difficult to hold ourselves to. I shine light on it because it must not be kept in the dark. Though the subjects in this variation of the experiment have a role in the process, they are effectively bystanders who are remaining silent. Yet, even in this variation of the Milgram experiment, 10 percent hold themselves sufficiently morally accountable to refuse to continue in their ancillary roles—refuse to be silent, complicit bystanders.

In our age of social media, sometimes one of these rare individuals feels called to raise public awareness of the abuses. Movements have been generated to label the origin of products, to avoid purchasing products from war-torn areas or those that are produced without fair and sustainable practices. Due to the amplifying powers of social media, tens of thousands pick up the cause and carry it forward. The producers of the products find it in their commercial interest to be responsive, and change does occur. This is another example in which you may not be the first to intelligently disobey, but you can support those who do when you recognize that they are standing up for doing the right thing.

Let's review some of the lessons we can draw from the variations to the basic experiment:

1. If you are uncomfortable about what you are told to do, speak up early and do not let your discomfort be dissipated by answers that are technical rather than moral.

2. If the order seems morally wrong or potentially illegal, unless there is immediate danger, require the order be given to you in writing; if the authority will not put the order in writing, do not implement it.

3. If the order conflicts with a higher set of values, rely on the authority of those values to make the decision for which you will be accountable.

4. If you are responsible for the ethical development of others, design opportunities to practice questioning technical orders that conflict with higher level moral orders.

5. If the action you are ordered to take will make its impact felt at a remote location or point in time, visualize that impact and whether it will conform to the morals and laws you are committed to upholding.

6. If you find yourself avoiding implementation of an order when the authority giving the order is not present, recognize you are not fully convinced the order is a correct one and question it more closely.

7. You are accountable if you implement a wrong order even if you feel bad about doing so and express disagreement with the order; only refusing to implement the order absolves you from complicity.

8. If you are an authority and disagree with the correctness or morality of the order of another authority, you are responsible for speaking up against the wrong orders and, thereby, helping others to do so.

9. Do not allow social politeness to keep you from speaking up clearly against morally incorrect orders from others, regardless of their position in the hierarchy and despite the discomfort of doing so.

10. If someone else resists a morally or operationally wrong order or systemic abuse before you do, support that person in refusing to comply with the order as given or in examining alternatives to the current practice.

There is more we can learn from Milgram, but let's leave him for a while and return to the inspiration for this book, the guide dog. What lessons will we find in the benign efforts to teach Intelligent Disobedience?

CHAPTER EIGHT

The Crucial Lessons from Guide Dog Training

O N A FIERCELY HOT DAY IN LATE JUNE, I drove onto the sixty-nine-acre campus of The Seeing Eye, Inc., in historic and well-preserved Morristown, New Jersey, to meet with its current president and CEO, Dr. James Kutsch. Jim Kutsch is one heck of a smart and likeable man and an erudite, thoughtful, and decisive executive. He holds a doctoral degree in computer science and developed one of the world's first screen-reading programs for the visually impaired. Jim is the first graduate of The Seeing Eye to become its president; Colby, his blonde Labrador retriever, stayed patiently in her bed in his office until needed to navigate the halls and campus.

You enter the main building on the campus through a walkway with paving stones donated by The Seeing Eye's supporters, which are mostly inscribed with love messages to the dogs that have transformed lives. Imagine spending nearly a decade of your life with a loyal dog who never left your side, waking or sleeping, and who tended to your safety as her first priority. Now imagine losing that dog, as the difference in human and canine life spans predicts you will. Here is one of the tributes engraved in stone:

FENIX—7-16-2006
STRENGTH WITHOUT INSOLENCE, COURAGE WITHOUT FEROCITY.
ALL THE VIRTUES OF MAN WITHOUT HIS VICES.

Temperamentally, it takes a special dog to become a guide dog. It needs both the placid disposition to spend hours quietly under the handler's feet in a restaurant, classroom, or airplane and the focus and energy to train and work in challenging environments, such as a busy commuter train station at rush hour.

When a puppy has been weaned, it is placed with a family who will raise it and help it become accustomed to the many social settings in which a guide dog will later find itself. That was the role of the woman in my class who had the dog she was training under her table.

What is so challenging about guide dog training? First, there is the need to focus. Your own dog walking down the street may be easily distracted by every passing movement and smell; a guide dog can never allow itself to be distracted. Of course, the dog needs to master obeying basic commands including forward, left, right, and stop, but that's the easy part. The challenging part is mastering when *not* to obey.

You may have imagined the prospect of becoming blind. Even so, it can be surprisingly difficult to imagine what it is really like to navigate the world without the use of your eyes. Let me once again ask you to do a mental exercise with me. Imagine your shifting emotional states as you read the next few paragraphs.

> You have lost the full use of your sight. Your world is filled with sounds and smells, shapes and textures, and a sense of spatial distances, but all visual cues are missing. You cannot tell if the driver in a car sees you before you step into the street, if a light has turned red or green by its color, or if workmen have dug up the street you are crossing. Two-ton behemoths we use by the millions for our transport whiz by with inches to spare, assuming that you can see them and will do your part to stay out of their way.
>
> You choose to live in an urban environment where there are many amenities within walking distance so you can be somewhat independent. You cannot drive, so suburbs and country settings leave you even more dependent on others for everyday needs. (As this book is being published, driverless cars are just becoming a reality. Technology may one day even supplant the trusted guide dog or re-create vision for the blind. At this time, however, the guide

dog remains an indispensable companion to thousands of those who have lost their sight.) The neighborhood you choose to live in becomes familiar to you; to get to the dry cleaners you walk four blocks straight ahead and two blocks to the right. You've had mobility training with a cane, so you are pretty good at maintaining your orientation and avoiding most obstacles with the sweeping back and forth motion of your cane. But there are always the unexpected obstacles—a branch that is lower than usual because of heavy rain, snow that has been piled against the sidewalk by plows, and, of course, the matter of crossing a street when cars can come speeding around a corner. After a few unpleasant encounters, near misses, and situations you found embarrassing or even humiliating, you begin limiting your outings and becoming more reclusive. This is not the path of a full life. Emotionally and socially, you are in danger of shutting down. You recognize you will need to do something different if you are to regain a sense of freedom to live your life the way you want.

In the hope of increasing your independence, you apply to a school that trains in the use of guide dogs. You are uncertain about this move—will you like having a dog with you every waking and sleeping moment, will you be able to care for it, will it make you stand out from other people even more than you do now? Despite these qualms, you feel cautiously excited when, after vigorous screening to assess your chances of success, you hear that you have been accepted to the school.

After four weeks of intensive training, morning to night, you and your new dog, Millie, return home. You have a new confidence that shows in your posture and your stride. The people who know you best are impressed by the transformation in so short a time. You are again ready to take that trip to the dry cleaners.

Walking confidently down the tree-lined street, Millie suddenly pulls you to the left instead of walking forward as commanded. What has happened? Unbeknown to you, but known to Millie, the *delicatessen en route to the cleaners has hung a sign announcing its lunch special. The sign is dangling six feet above the ground, making it easy for Millie to pass under with plenty of headroom to spare. But you are six-feet-two and would get a rude jar and a nasty gash if Millie had kept going straight as commanded. How did Millie know to avoid that sign, which was no danger to her, and to firmly pull you in a different direction than you instructed? How did Millie learn this situational awareness and Intelligent Disobedience?*

This is where Dave Johnson comes in. Dave is director of instruction and training at The Seeing Eye. He oversees the selection and training of 250 dogs at any given time, with the help of two dozen trainers who have each spent years learning their craft. Dave is responsible for the selection, instruction, and post-graduate support for twelve groups of blind students a year, with up to twenty-four students in each month-long class. He has been with The Seeing Eye for twenty-eight years. It is safe to say that he is as knowledgeable as anyone in his field.

Dave and Jim took me, Colby, and another small Labrador retriever to the very beautiful Morristown train station to demonstrate how Intelligent Disobedience works. Dave parked the van in a handicap spot, and we all disembarked. Normally, when the train pulls in, Dave would give the command "forward," and the dog would find the nearest open doorway and lead him through it. In this case, the train hadn't arrived. When he commanded the dog to go forward toward the edge of the platform, instead of obeying she did an about face and pulled him decisively away from it. This is known as a "counter-pull." Those of us who work in hierarchical settings should take note: *counter-pull* may be a good term for us to adopt when the leader is about to step off the edge into whatever danger he or she is unaware of. It looks like insubordination but, in fact, a counter-pull may be lifesaving!

The Leader Sets the Direction

All guide dog training starts with a basic principle: the leader sets the direction and the guide dog finds a safe way to get there.

The day Jim and Dave and I met, the temperature was touching a hundred degrees. It was too hot to ask the dog to work on the street where the pavement would burn the pads of her feet. Dave described what we would have seen if he worked the dog at the crossing.

The dog is trained to stop at every intersection and wait for the next command, which may be "forward" or "left" or "right." Both the leader and the dog maintain situational awareness through the senses available to them. The dog can see but does not see colors the way we do; it cannot tell when a light has turned from red to green. The human listens to the environment and knows from the sounds of people and cars, or low audibles built into the system, when the light has changed and it is apparently safe to cross. At that point the leader gives the forward command. The dog must decide if it is safe to obey it. At just that moment, a fast-moving messenger bike may be turning sharply around the corner! The dog disregards, or actually overrides the command, and stays put. It may be another cycle of the light before it is safe to cross the street.

Now here's where we who are interested in Intelligent Disobedience need to pay close attention. How does Dave train his dogs in this faculty, which one observer called "the higher mathematics of dog training"? Which aspects of that training are transferrable to human training and education? What are the precise points that make it successful?

The first thing to know is that there is a great emphasis on praise. When the dog successfully executes any new skill it is learning, or applies that skill deftly, it is given hearty praise, verbally and at times physically. This is the foundation of building confidence and trust: praise when well deserved.

But praise alone is an incomplete tool kit for teaching the full range of behaviors needed to safely serve as a human's eyes. There is no margin for error. If guide dogs occasionally stepped in front of an oncoming car, there would be no Seeing Eye—the risks would be too great. A complementary set of tools must be used to ensure that the training is completely effective. That is a higher bar of effectiveness than most of us ever have to meet.

In addition to the harness and rigid handle that permit clear communication in both directions between the guide dog and the human handler (note the derivation), there is also a leash. The leash can be utilized to correct the dog when it makes an error. The trainer or the blind handler can yank firmly on the leash to correct the dog, while using the expression "phooey" (phooey is an expression of displeasure used for its distinctiveness—"no" is used too frequently in human interaction and can confuse the dog). This may sound very ho-hum to the reader. What's new here, positive and negative reinforcement? We all know about the impact of that on behavior, whether or not we apply it as consistently as we should. Is that all there is to it?

The Elements of
Intelligent Disobedience Training

Jim had told me there is no "secret sauce" to Intelligent Disobedience training, but I think there are at least some essential ingredients that go into that sauce. Dave shared the exact application of positive and negative reinforcement that makes it effective in guide dog training.

When the dog does something requiring a "phooey" correction you *always* take it back to the starting point of that action and let it go through the sequence again, so it has a chance to do it right. If it does it right, you give it its due praise. In fact, and this is very important, you give it three chances to do it right. If the dog still doesn't "get it," it is equally important that you cease trying to teach that behavior that day. If not, you risk making the dog afraid, and at that point it cannot serve as a guide dog. This methodology of always allowing three times to get it right, whatever the "it" is, is an excellent point for any educator, trainer, coach, or manager to bear in mind. We are working toward competence, not failure and not anxiety!

The dog also must experience the consequence of obeying a command it should not. The train platform in Morristown is mostly very low, perhaps a foot above the rail bed, except for the short piece that is elevated to accommodate the lifts needed to bring passengers in wheelchairs aboard. If Dave were training a dog in Intelligent Disobedience on the platform, and it followed a "forward" command when it should not have, Dave will do a controlled stumble over the low edge while making unpleasant sounds and pulling the dog down with him. No one gets hurt, but it's no fun either. The dog now has an experience of the consequences both to herself and to her human partner of obeying in that situation.

This technique is extended to crossing the street. Another trainer is at the wheel of a car that is coming around the corner. If Dave gives the "forward" command and the dog obeys, the car gently sideswipes him. Exaggerating the impact, Dave again stumbles, groans, and pulls the dog with him. No one is hurt, but no one is happy.

What's interesting to me here is that once again we have the field of obedience and disobedience being explored and taught through actors and consequences. Milgram used his actors to elicit and study subjects' responses. Dave uses his to mold those responses. Crew Resource Management training stages simulations to increase situational awareness and assertiveness when alerting authority to potential risks. One parallel we can take away is the value of staging and rehearsing scenarios in teaching Intelligent Disobedience.

These scenarios become increasingly complex. Dave and his trainers will create "box traps" for the dogs. They set up obstacles— boards, fences, barrels—along routes the dog usually walks. Following the "forward" command unexpectedly puts the dog and his human charge into a box. It is now up to the sighted partner, the guide dog, to problem solve. *It is not enough to simply disobey.*

To trust the well-being of a blind student to the dog requires that the training create dogs that can and will problem solve, not just for themselves, but for the team. If the dog goes over the barriers, which might work well for it but not for a blind person, it will get a "phooey" and be given three chances to develop a response that is safe and effective for both of them. If we are interested in developing Intelligent Disobedience in humans, we, too, will need to do so in ways that foster problem solving.

Nor is it acceptable when confronted with these obstacles and dangers for the dog to dither before problem solving. Dog dithering may take the form of prolonged sniffing or scratching. Although this instinctive behavior may calm its own anxiety in an unexpected situation, it does nothing toward getting the team out of the box. In animal training, this is referred to as displacement behavior. In humans, we call it procrastination. Faced with a tough decision to make? Let's take a coffee break or check our email instead. Recognizing procrastination as displacement behavior is another piece of Intelligent Disobedience training we can transfer.

If the copilot is unsure whether to wait for instructions or to remind the surly air traffic controller that the plane is getting dangerously low on fuel, as occurred with Avianca Flight 52 over New York City in 1990, he may resort to rechecking other settings. That may help control his anxiety, but his focus should stay on getting landing permission immediately to avoid the crash and the seventy-three fatalities that resulted. Most of us can relate to displacement behavior. We may get away with it as civilians making low-consequence decisions. Guide dogs, like pilots, firefighters, war fighters, or emergency room personnel, don't have that luxury. In the dog's case, the displacement behavior earns another sharp "phooey."

The principles of praise, correction, and giving the dog three chances to solve a problem are applied in this situation until the dog demonstrates understanding of what is expected of her and she leads her human partner out of the box, whether that day or, if necessary, in a subsequent day's training.

When they are safely out of the box, the lead returns to the human. Switching the lead and follow roles, and then handing back the lead role to the human when the danger is past, is an aspect of the natural flow between Intelligent Disobedience and obedience, another salient point in human leader-follower relationships.

When the guide dog becomes confident in this role, she will be presented with more difficult constructed problems to solve. Perhaps it will be night, and flashing lights and distracting street-life sounds will be added. Although she has learned not to consciously walk into box traps, the next one isn't as obvious. Once in it, she needs even greater focus to problem solve a way out of it. Increasing the complexity of simulations is a principle that transfers well to effectively inculcating Intelligent Disobedience in humans.

Dave and Jim report another sequence that I think contains parallels for our purposes. Initially, the dogs do or don't do the expected behaviors because of the praise and corrections they receive. This is similar to the literature on the early stages of moral reasoning and ethical behavior in humans, in which children focus on doing things to avoid punishment and seek gratification.

At some point, guide dogs seem to progress beyond this stage to an intense awareness of the well-being, and the risks to that well-being, of the human with whom they have developed a trusting, even loving, relationship. There is no prescribed technique for achieving this transition; it is a manifestation of the bond that occurs through continuous mutual respect and care. I venture to identify this as another essential ingredient in the "secret sauce." The human is caring for the guide dog's needs every day through feeding, watering, grooming, exercise, and elimination routines, heartfelt praise, affection, and companionship. The guide dog forms an understanding that its work in life is the care of this precious human being. As Jim Kutsch says, he is this dog's pack.

At the risk of stretching the analogy too far, it seems as if the guide dog is moving from the lower levels of moral reasoning observed in human development to higher levels. The guide dog's attention moves from avoiding punishment or seeking praise for herself and becomes focused on the well-being of her human partner without any explicit directions to do so. There are numerous stories of guide dogs initiating behavior to protect their human partner when the human is unaware of danger. This is the fruit of any relationship in which there is mutual respect and caring—valuing the well-being of the other as much as one's own and, at times, even more so.

In service dog training, this is equally true. In addition to guide dogs, there are many other types of service dogs. Different schools and trainers specialize in different competencies, such as hearing dogs, or mobility dogs. Lydia Wade was the founder of the nonprofit group Blue Ridge Assistance Dogs. Her service dogs were trained to assist individuals with limited mobility or those who had medical conditions such as diabetes or epilepsy that made them prone to seizures or comas. Lydia tells numerous stories of dogs she trained and placed that have prevented someone from walking down a flight of stairs when the individual was showing signs of fainting or of an impending seizure. The dog has literally blocked them moving forward. This is proactive disobedience. Not just failing to obey a dangerous command, but physically stopping the human's own action to protect him or her from harm. Lydia, too, observes this growing out of the bond between dog and human and each dog finding its own way to warn against harm or to actively prevent it.

How Leaders Encourage or Discourage Intelligent Disobedience

Of course, the effectiveness of Intelligent Disobedience depends in part on the response of the authority that is being disobeyed. Another ingredient to the sauce!

The cofounder of The Seeing Eye, Inc., Morris Frank, and others tell stories of when they failed to respect a guide dog's disobedience and sufficiently examine the reasons that might lay behind it before acting. Overriding the disobedience usually resulted in a nasty thump, or worse, from something the dog was protecting against.

Why were the dog's warnings not heeded? This is an important question to explore if Intelligent Disobedience is to make a difference when it is employed.

We all proceed through life with mental maps of what we believe the situation to be as we pass from one situation to another. These do not depend on sight; they are the interior maps we create to help us make choices from among the moves available to us in any given circumstance. Once we form a map, it is hard for us to realize it may be incorrect and to imagine alternative scenarios. This is as dangerous as using ocean navigation charts that are out of date and don't show recent shifts in the seafloor, or following maps in our satellite-based navigation device that don't show current road closures. We could call this a blind spot, but it is even worse—*it is a false picture of reality.* That is why in creative problem solving and brainstorming exercises we strive to suspend judgment until we have entertained a range of plausible scenarios and responses to them. The initial scenario we envision may be woefully wrong and our initial responses significantly inferior to others we can generate.

Whether leaders are physically blind or metaphorically blind, they need to train themselves to be alert for and responsive to acts of Intelligent Disobedience. Why is a trusted dog, or a loyal aide, or a well-regarded employee disobeying an instruction? Betty Vinson might have taken a stand and refused to manipulate WorldCom's monthly financial reports. That would have been Intelligent Disobedience. But her leaders would have needed the instinct or training to allow her refusal to impact them. The effective response would have been,

> *If this loyal and competent employee is refusing to comply with the request, perhaps we should examine alternatives before proceeding.*

Only then might disaster have been averted.

Jim Kutsch reports that a significant barrier to guide dogs becoming fully proficient is when the handler is not completely blind. Most residents at The Seeing Eye who are being trained to work with their guide dog have no sight; a few are legally blind but have some degree of sight. The tendency of this latter group is to use their limited sight to discern barriers on their own and take evasive action. The dog quickly recognizes the human is not depending on it for this function. Sooner or later, the team is out for a stroll when the evening light is disappearing, or the individual's eyesight has deteriorated further, and the handler can't see a low limb before crashing into it. He is annoyed the dog didn't steer him out of harm's way, not realizing that he has trained the dog that it wasn't necessary to do so. Jim's advice to the partially sighted is to use that gift of sight to enjoy the beauty of their surroundings that they still have the pleasure of seeing—and to let the dog do the navigating. This takes self-awareness and self-discipline.

I hope that any organizational leaders reading this have paid attention to the last point. If your staff starts assuming that you surely see the pitfalls they see, they will not develop the habit of checking and alerting you to what they observe. We have already seen the tragic results of that dynamic from our examination of the aviation industry prior to the introduction of Crew Resource Management training.

Jim Kutsch, Dave Johnson, and I sat around Jim's conference table discussing the implications of Intelligent Disobedience. I was drawing them into my agenda for translating the lessons of guide dog training to human training, particularly for youth. Dave's expression grew more serious as he shared his thoughts with us.

He and his wife felt it would be good for their fourteen-year-old son to go to an outdoors camp in Canada to learn a range of skills and life lessons. They got their son's agreement and were ready to submit the camp application and processing fee. That day, Dave read in the paper that Jerry Sandusky, the famed assistant football coach at Penn State University, had been arrested on multiple charges of child molestation. Dave confided his concerns to his wife: *"How can we send our son away for three weeks into the care of strange men in an isolated setting?"* This troubled him, but Dave is a strong individual who knows you can't hide from life—trouble can come unexpectedly from anywhere, including from those you think you know, like Jerry Sandusky.

When the time came for Dave's son to leave for camp, Dave decided he needed to sit him down and give him a direct talk about how to handle himself in troubling situations that might arise with other campers or counselors, including drugs, alcohol, smoking, or sexual advances. It was a good talk, preparing his son to listen to his own discomfort in situations, to recognize his own values, and to take his own stand, regardless of whether others did so or not. Dave also knew he had to be careful to warn his son about the potential of danger without scaring him about it. This was the same line Dave walked with training his dogs in Intelligent Disobedience.

I complimented Dave on his willingness to have a difficult talk with his son and to do so while remaining sensitive to the risks the talk itself held. I also pointed out that having this conversation the evening before his son's departure would not necessarily be sufficient to equip him to take the right action in a given situation. Without wanting to scare Dave any more than he wanted to scare his son, having that talk at the eleventh hour seemed equivalent to giving a guide dog one lesson in Intelligent Disobedience and expecting it to perform thereafter when under pressure.

I asked Dave, somewhat rhetorically, if he could envision how society might instill the capacity his son needed through training activities woven into the school curriculum at different ages? Neither Dave nor Jim nor I came up with a blueprint for doing this during the conversation, but I appreciated their willingness to join me in considering the linkages between canine and human Intelligent Disobedience.

Having time to reflect on our conversation, I am better prepared now to integrate what I learned at The Seeing Eye with the material we have already covered in this book. There are two major themes emerging that hold promise for being woven together.

The first theme goes back to Stanley Milgram's experiments. It is *the primacy of social context*. Milgram didn't try to identify what type of personality was more likely to disobey destructive orders; nor did he speculate on what type of training might create the capacity for resistance. Milgram focused on the social context of his core experiment and each of its variations. He observed the ways in which the social context can be constructed to increase or decrease the incidence of compliance to orders that violate standards of human decency. From these variations we learned the impact on obedience of physical proximity to authority, of authorities disagreeing with one another, of peers refusing to comply with orders, and of other related social factors. These are important lessons. We saw the effectiveness of these variations at reducing harmful obedience from two-thirds of the population to as little as 10 percent or less. We must bear these lessons in mind when designing activities that hold potential for the misuse of power.

The second theme is *the power of training*. It runs through various scenarios we have examined, such as the captain who drilled the lieutenant on saying "That's BS, sir!" until he could do it under stress, through the Crew Resource Management training on speaking assertively to command, through the nursing training that today places more emphasis on how to speak up to reduce physician mistakes, right through to guide dog training. Jim Kutsch made the point clearly: it is repetitive training, well done, that ensures the dog will make the right choice between obeying and disobeying in any given situation.

It is our good fortune that these two themes are not mutually exclusive. They are complementary. This is heartening to realize. Together they hold the potential for creating cultures in which the norm is to discern between appropriate and inappropriate obedience.

Let's summarize lessons we have distilled from our observations of guide dog training that can transfer to developing human capacity for Intelligent Disobedience.

1. Intelligent Disobedience can be developed through carefully designed training and practice.

2. Start with simple simulations in which Intelligent Disobedience is called for and work toward more complex situations.

3. Emphasize praise for appropriate acts of Intelligent Disobedience during practice sessions.

4. If the individual fails to appropriately display Intelligent Disobedience in a simulation, give the individual a sense of the adverse consequences that can befall the team.

5. If the individual doesn't display an Intelligent Disobedience response when he or she should, take the simulation back to the beginning and give the individual another try; build confidence.

6. Allow the individual being trained three tries to generate an effective Intelligent Disobedience response in a given situation; if the individual doesn't get it right by then, cease further training that day and pick it up another day soon afterward.

7. In addition to practicing not obeying a poor or dangerous command, practice the equivalent of a counter-pull to bring the leader to a safer position.

8. Create more complex practice scenarios in which the individual not only exerts Intelligent Disobedience but also creatively finds alternative solutions to meet the legitimate needs of the authority.

9. When the danger has been avoided, have the follower hand the lead role back to the authorized leader.

10. Have the individual practice the lead role in a scenario he thinks he understands. Have the follower take an action that doesn't conform to that understanding but is an act of Intelligent Disobedience. Debrief the exercise for what the individual in the lead will do in future situations to pay better attention to the follower.

This will be a learning experience for everyone involved—the simulation designers, the facilitators, those in the role plays, and those measuring the impact of the training. The task is to create a body of research and experience from which we learn effective ways at different ages, and in different cultures, to impart the awareness and skills that comprise Intelligent Disobedience.

CHAPTER NINE

The Price of Teaching Obedience Too Well

UNFORTUNATELY, THERE IS VIRTUALLY no Intelligent Disobedience training in human school systems. We will examine the contribution this omission makes to the significant problem of misplaced obedience. First, let's witness the dramatic and shocking results of failing to instill Intelligent Disobedience in our sons and daughters. I must warn you, what follows is disturbing.[1]

In 2004, an eighteen-year-old girl named Louise Ogborn went to work for a McDonald's fast-food restaurant in Mount Washington, Kentucky. Mount Washington is small-town America, which we like to think of as representing the best of traditional American values. She was a "good child," with no history of trouble in school or with the law. On April 9th, her eighteen years of being well behaved and compliant rebounded on her in a way that left her emotionally scarred for years.

That evening, the assistant manager on duty at the McDonald's, Donna Jean Summers, fifty-one years old, got a disturbing telephone call from "Officer Scott." Officer Scott told her that a customer had accused a female employee of stealing her purse. The description he gave matched that of Louise Ogborn.

Scott instructed Summers that Louise needed to be searched. He offered two choices: Louise could be arrested and taken to police headquarters and searched there, or Donna could search her at the restaurant under his directions. Scott told her that corporate had approved the action. It seemed better to Summers, perhaps more humane, to conduct the search on the premises. Following Scott's directions, she took Louise to a store room in the back of the restaurant, locked the door, and had Louise remove each item of her clothing so it could be shaken for hidden stolen goods and then put in a bag. Louise obeyed and was soon naked, distraught, and crying.

What then proceeds defies imagination. Summers followed Scott's detailed orders for an hour. He said he would get to the restaurant as soon as he could to collect the items of clothing. Summers had to get back to work. It was dinner time, and the restaurant was busy. Scott said Louise needed to be detained a little longer and asked if Summers had a husband who could continue to watch her? She called her boyfriend, "Wes" Nix Jr., and told him to come in to help with "a situation." He did as asked, and for the next two hours followed Scott's increasingly sadistic telephone instructions. These began with having Louise do jumping jacks while unclothed to "see if anything fell out." They proceeded to overt acts of sexual abuse at the instructions of the "police officer" caller. Louise tearfully pleaded to be let go but continued to comply with the humiliating orders. When Summers came in periodically to check on the situation, Nix was instructed by Scott to have Louise cover herself with a small apron.

The ordeal continued until Scott told Summers to bring in another man to replace Nix. She called in Thomas Simms, a fifty-eight-year-old maintenance man who did odd jobs for the restaurant. Scott told Simms to have Louise drop the apron and describe her. Simms, a ninth-grade dropout, refused because "it didn't seem right." It was only then, some four hours later, that Summers also realized something was not right and called her manager who knew nothing about the matter. Apparently mortified by her gullibility, Summers let the traumatized Louise Ogborn dress and leave the storage room.

Of course, Scott was not a police officer. He had mastered the authoritative tone and language of police officers and did enough research on the locality to produce a thin patina of credibility. There are so many things wrong with this story (many more than I have included here, not wishing to spread the true but sensational account further) that it is hard to accept its veracity. There are several reasons why we must tell the story.

The first is that the entire ordeal was recorded on the security camera in the storage room. The details are not reconstructed. The entire gruesome ordeal is on record. This is the "black box" of an airplane crash, with video added.

The second reason is that nearly seventy other establishments in more than thirty states, mostly fast-food restaurants (including seventeen other McDonald's restaurants), were successfully targeted by the same caller. Investigators found that many other restaurant managers he contacted refused to obey, as we would suspect based on the lower compliance rate Milgram found when the authority was remote and phoning in his instructions. That still leaves seventy restaurants in which employees obeyed this faceless voice on the phone claiming to be a police officer. Unlike in the Milgram experiments, his ability to extract compliance didn't even depend on a uniform as a symbol of authority. The acts the targeted managers obediently performed on fellow employees were varied, but of the same humiliating and outrageous nature and mostly in small-town America.

Once again we are left wondering, *How does this grossly misplaced obedience to authority occur and what do we do about it?*

Let's begin with the assistant manager, Donna Jean Summers. Her case is problematic. Was she a victim or a perpetrator? This is the classic question concerning obedience, addressed at Nuremberg, WorldCom, and elsewhere. Because she became a defendant in a case of "unlawful imprisonment" to determine her culpability, her testimony and interviews became guarded and self-protective, and thus do not shed reliable light on her frame of mind. It has been reported that she had already received a reprimand on an unrelated matter from management. This may have reinforced a disposition to cooperate with a "management-approved investigation." But we are speculating here.

What we do know is that we saw her on the video at points in the strip search consoling Louise Ogborn. Like the subjects in the Milgram experiments, complying with these orders was not something she enjoyed doing. This was a case of blind compliance to perceived authority despite the hurt she was causing. By this standard, which must be the standard we use, she is an agent of the perpetrator and thus complicit in the shocking wrongdoing.

We also know that at one point, before Nix was brought in, a twenty-seven-year-old male employee named Jason Bradlee was instructed to help Summers follow the caller's instructions. We see Bradlee say, "This is BS" and refuse to follow the instructions. This is interesting for a number of reasons. First, like the soldier at Abu Ghraib who refused to obey the order to apply enhanced interrogation techniques, Bradlee kept himself from perpetrating the acts, but he did not stop them. He walked out of the storage room but did not notify the police. Despite his Intelligent Disobedience, authority and social context may have further constrained his ethical decision making. It is one thing to disobey an outrageous order, another for a young minority male to blow the whistle on an older white female supervisor.

The second reason Bradlee's refusal to follow Scott's orders is instructive is that the refusal to comply by another human being was insufficient to overcome Summers's thrall to perceived authority. Perhaps this was because Bradlee was young and black in rural Kentucky or perhaps she was like many in Milgram's experiments who kept administering shocks after one other person refused to continue with the experiment and stopped only when a second person joined in the resistance.

In the wake of these dismaying events, litigation and counter-litigation followed among the parties. Some people see Summers as victim, others as perpetrator; in reality she was both. Against the prosecutor's recommendation for a harsher sentence, she received one year probation for unlawful imprisonment, a lenient outcome but nevertheless an indelible stain on her professional record. She, in turn, sued McDonald's for failing to notify her of the instances of the multiple fraudulent police calls to other McDonald's restaurants. She was awarded several hundred thousand dollars compensation for the ordeal. The clear victim, Louise Ogborn, was awarded several million dollars. We will return to Louise shortly.

Summers's forty-two-year-old boyfriend, "Wes" Nix Jr., initially fit into the role of obeying authority that we saw in the Milgram experiments. Over the two hours in which he executed Scott's orders, however, his behavior transformed into that documented in the famous behavioral experiment conducted by Dr. Philip Zimbardo at Stanford University, which became known as the Stanford Prison Experiment and is described in the foreword to this book by Dr. Zimbardo. To refresh, in these experiments subjects were divided into two groups—guards and prisoners. Over the course of six days, the behavior of the guards became sadistic and physically abusive, requiring the experiment to be stopped for ethical reasons.

Unfortunately, Nix's deterioration into sadistic guard behavior occurred in hours rather than days, and there was no experimenter to stop the behavior. Scott ordered increased abuse of the naked Ogborn, including harsh spankings and oral sex. He was criminally prosecuted and received a five-year sentence. If he were the only one to have followed "Scott's" perverse orders to this degree, we would be tempted to dismiss his actions as a perverse anomaly. That is what we usually do in cases of destructive obedience. It is more comfortable to think of outrageous obedience as an aberration. Yet, according to a 2004 article in the *Louisville Courier-Journal*, strip searches were conducted at virtually all of the seventy documented locations. At least thirteen other people who executed them were charged with crimes, and seven were convicted as of the writing of that article. Unfortunately, this was not the depraved action of an isolated deviant individual; it is one more example of a social phenomenon of misplaced obedience.

What of "Officer Scott"? It took a long time to put together the pieces of these widely distributed events. Some restaurants didn't report the events out of fear of the negative publicity, and some police departments couldn't figure out under what category to file the reports when they were made. They weren't even sure if the caller had committed an actionable crime. What would the crime be? Calling store managers over the phone and ordering them, but not coercing them, to perform bizarre actions, which they then complied with? The most tangible offense was impersonating a police officer, though he did so with no false uniform, badge, or other identification.

Eventually, through coordinated detective work among state law enforcement agencies, calling cards used for several of these deplorable events were traced back to a thirty-eight-year-old man, David R. Stewart, who purchased them in Florida, where he lived. Stewart claimed innocence, but police found incriminating evidence including, for example, a card with a call placed to a restaurant in Idaho Falls on the day its manager had complied with fraudulent "police orders." Stewart was employed as a security officer with Corrections Corporation of America, a private prison company. When identified as the suspect, he was a guard on the swing shift of the Bay Correctional Facility.

If Stewart was indeed the perpetrator, he was an extreme example of the Stanford Prison experiment. Given the phone-based communications, however, it was difficult to categorize the crime and make it stick. The violations he was charged with are reported to have carried half the potential prison time of the charges levied against Nix. Unlike Nix, he was acquitted in trial for lack of evidence and served no jail time. The difference between Nix's fate and Stewart's provides us with one more cautionary tale about obeying when one should refuse.

This brings us to the undisputed victim of the case, Louise Ogborn. Her humiliation and great distress are clearly visible on security tapes. Why did Louise become the victim? Without in any way shifting blame from the perpetrators to Louise, we need to examine her own acts of obedience and how culture colludes to make many of us prone to inappropriate obedience.

Why Did You Follow the Instructions?

In a televised interview after the event, Louise Ogborn was asked why she followed the instructions Summers, and then Nix, relayed to her from "Officer Scott"? Her response is almost heartbreaking. Those who care most about her are the reason she gives for obeying her tormentors.

> *"My parents taught me when an adult tells you to do something, you don't argue. If someone swipes you on the hand you listen."*

This is the unrecognized conundrum faced by all parents: teach your children to obey their elders; teach it with the gravitas of "honor your father and mother"; teach them to be polite, respectful, and obedient. This is good, loving advice in a world in which adults are stewards of learned wisdom and protectors of the social order.

But sometimes adults are priests who prey on boys, or coaches who violate them, or relatives who take sexual liberties, or teachers who duct-tape them to a chair, or supervisors who tell them to strip in a backroom of a fast-food restaurant.

> *"My parents taught me when an adult tells you to do something, you don't argue."*

You don't argue. You silence your voice. You do not have the right to speak up assertively in noncompliance.

> *"If someone swipes you on the hand you listen."*

Louise's family goes further than many; if the command is reinforced physically you pay extra attention, you are extra-obedient.

Surely, they did not envision their injunction against speaking back being applied in a nightmare like Louise's. Parents routinely warn their children against the dangers of following strangers; they hardly ever warn against refusing instructions from pillars of the family or the community.

Louise was eighteen years old, nearly finished with high school. She was no longer a child. Surely, these teachings should have long since been put into context. Clearly, they were not.

In testimony Louise said,

"I was scared because they were a higher authority than me."

Fear of a higher authority as we have seen is not limited to children or teenagers. It is as ubiquitous as it is dangerous. But how does this occur, and what purpose does it serve?

Evolutionary genetics postulates that obedience to authority became a survival trait of our species.[2] With the capacity to mobilize tens of thousands of individuals in coordinated activity, our species was able to accomplish feats never approached by small bands of humans. Massive armies could be raised and deployed, giving groups military protection or advantage. The dark side of this coin was that millions of people could be mobilized in support of megalomaniacs who lead their people to destruction. As humanity came through the horrors of two world wars, researchers like Milgram and Zimbardo tried to plumb the behavioral nature accounting for mass obedience to destructive uses of authority. They documented that the behaviors emerged not just in a small sliver of humanity, but in the majority of human beings when placed in circumstances that support these behaviors.

Yet, even in the field of genetics, genes are not the only factor recognized for contributing to behavior. Environmental factors play a role in determining which genes are expressed and which remain dormant. What are the environmental factors that kept obedience to authority active in Louise in the face of the outrageous abuse of authority? In addition to her family, who else impressed on her that obeying adults was a cardinal rule? What environmental factors reinforced this conditioning as she got older? What kept these child-hood rules so firmly in place when she should have been making her transition to adulthood?

It is critical we examine this if we are ever going to get to the root of the problem. We will always be remediating this at the professional level of soldier, flight crew, accountant, nurse if we do not create a conscious pathway for young people to complete their education with the ability to make reasoned moral distinctions and the capacity to stand by them. If you are a working adult who is reading this for its application to your organization, remember that I am also writing to you as a current or future parent, or the concerned relative of young people. We must understand how we develop those who will be future political and corporate citizens in whom much trust is placed.

In every society and age, the relevant environmental factors vary. In traditional societies, the socialization may be achieved through the whole tribe or village tutoring the young in the norms of tribal life. In an agricultural society, the dominant shaping may occur in the months working side by side with elders in the fields during plant-ing and harvest. In militaristic societies, training youth in the arts of the warrior may begin early and be a consistent feature of child rear-ing. In virtually every society, though, the environmental factors that reinforce obedience are there. Until we identify and understand those factors in our own culture, we cannot successfully introduce balanc-ing factors that dramatically change the percentages of destructive obedience that Milgram documented.

Three environmental factors mentioned in relation to Louise Ogborn were church, Girl Scouts, and school. The teachings of church and Scouts undoubtedly reinforced natural tendencies to obey authority. But together they represent a small fraction of the time Louise spent in that ubiquitous institution of our contemporary society—school. With the exception of the small home-school move-ment, our children spend the largest part of their waking lives out-side the home, in public, private, or parochial schools, from the time they are four or five years old, or even younger, until they are at least Louise's age. What is it about school, where students are supposed to learn to think and form their own perspectives, that reinforces unquestioning obedience to authority?

Compliance and Classroom Management

Mount Washington, Kentucky, is in Bullitt County. On page 5 of the Bullitt County Public Schools Code of Student Behavior and Discipline, 2011–2102 it states:

> *Among student responsibilities: To obey the rules and regulations of the Board of Education and/or school administrators and to question them only for explanation not in an argumentative context.*
>
> *To exercise courtesy and reason at all times, to accept just punishment, to avoid unreasonable appeals, and to refrain from making false accusations.*

It is reasonable to assume that this language or language similar to it existed in the 2003 version of the code as well. We cannot know for sure that Louise Ogborn was required to read the code or, if she did read it, that it directly affected her thinking or behavior. But it does give us insight into the culture of the Bullitt County school system, with its emphasis on student obedience, disapproval of students arguing with authority, expectation of accepting punishment deemed just by authority, and implicitly warning that accusations against authority may raise questions of false witness. It is not my intention to single out Bullitt County, but rather to use it as representative of the broad education system. One of the recent alumni from Teach for America who read this story, found Bullitt County's policies not unusual and reported the exercise of authority to be harsher in other regions with which he was familiar.

In the context of the Ogborn case, it is surprising to me that this language was not rewritten by 2010 to be more sensitive in response to the event. But we cannot be entirely unsympathetic to the Bullitt County Board of Education for setting a stern tone regarding student behavior. As every teacher or close friend or family member of a teacher knows, managing students' behavior in a classroom is the difference between making that chosen career satisfying and escaping from it as soon as possible. A former teacher who left the field to become a caterer explained her reason succinctly: "Green beans don't talk back." Consider the desperation that must have preceded the decision of the teacher we met earlier to duct-tape her misbehaving student to his chair!

One of the friends I have made in my twenty-year journey through the subject of leading and following is Marty Krovetz. Marty is a thoughtful, well-spoken man whose career took him to a position of high school principal for fourteen years. He has authored or coauthored three books on education including *Collaborative Teacher Leadership: How Teachers Can Foster Equitable Schools* (2006, with Gilberto Arriaza) and *Powerful Partnerships: A Handbook for Principals Mentoring Assistant Principals* (2008, with Gary Bloom). In both of these books, Marty devotes a chapter to following courageously. In the handbook, this meant giving ardent support to one's principal while being equally willing to "speak truth to power" if the principal's blind spots were hurting the school's capacity to fulfill its mission. I reached out to Marty to thank him for incorporating my work in his own important work.

Over the years Marty and I have had several valuable conversations. A few years ago we ran a pilot project together to introduce the concepts of courageous followership to middle school students. The students had identified that their school and its heavily immigrant population were significantly under-resourced in technology relative to other schools in their district that were primarily serving the majority population. Under the guidance of their teachers, the students organized themselves into groups, each with a specific responsibility for mounting a campaign to remedy this disparity.

They had their share of successes and setbacks as is natural in activist campaigns, and displayed a fine appreciation for the principles of courageous followership.

Given our history together, I turned to Marty for any experience he could share with me on how Intelligent Disobedience was taught in schools. He could not identify any experiences or resources to share with me. I rephrased my question and asked him for widely used templates for obtaining obedience in classroom management. Marty directed me to two resources.

The first is a book and program developed by Dr. Frederic H. Jones called *Tools for Teaching*. Jones's books, videos, and DVDs have won awards from a number of well-regarded education and publishing bodies. Endorsements come from around the United States, including from Joe Burke, an assistant school superintendent in Jefferson County, which borders Bullitt County, where Louise Ogborn went to school.

> *"Tools for Teaching will be vital to the culture of our high schools for years to come. More than a classroom management system, these tools have strengthened every other instructional initiative we have implemented."*

The second is a book and program developed by Lee Canter called *Lee Canter's Classroom Management for Academic Success*. According to the information on the back cover of the book, Lee Canter and his staff have trained more than 1.5 million teachers. The book can be supplemented with a number of other resources entitled *Assertive Discipline, Assertive Discipline Workbook (K–6), Assertive Discipline Workbook (7–12)*, and *accompanying Assertive Discipline* videos for each age group.

Both Jones's and Cantor's books are large format, coming in at just under or over three hundred pages. Marty preferred Jones's methods to Canter's. As I read through each, I paid attention to why that would be so. It became clear that Jones's book starts with a series of very practical strategies that enhance classroom learning, which he sees as setting the foundation for good classroom management. Canter's book dives right into classroom management and more or less ignores learning strategies, presumably because this is just one of some forty books on education that he has written.

Nevertheless, when the picture was complete, there was not as much daylight between Jones's classroom management strategies and Canter's as I had gotten the impression there would be from Marty's description. Both were recipes for managing student behavior down to the last iota of movement and speech. I am going to ask you, the reader, to join me in a "deep dive" into this subject because doing so is necessary for revealing the intensity of obedience training that is not otherwise obvious to us. If you are a classroom teacher, you may be very familiar with this material, in which case I am going to ask you to revisit it from the perspective of its meta-effect on obedience conditioning.

Before I go into details of these instruction manuals, and the implications of these and others like them about teaching obedience *too well*, let me express sympathy for what they are each trying to accomplish. Let's use another imagination exercise to get some emotional reality of what classroom teachers are up against every day.

Imagine yourself as a twenty-five-year-old teacher. You became a teacher with the idea of helping young people develop their capacity for a well-lived life. Perhaps you are part of Teach for America. Perhaps you are in an inner-city school with many young children from single parent or foster homes, or teenagers who have had to learn to fend for themselves in difficult neighborhoods. Perhaps you are teaching in a suburban or rural school in which students ride the bus each way for a half hour or more and come home when their parent or parents are still at work.

Imagine the thirty or so different personalities in your classroom—some from homes in which discipline was stern, others from homes in which frazzled parents never enforced the threats they were constantly making to curb unwanted behavior. Some of the students in your classroom have learned to dominate others to get along in the world, some have learned to retreat into their shells and not talk very much, some are quick mentally and get easily bored, others are just as easily confused and lost by the assignments you give them.

In the earlier grades, you may have the students for all or much of the day in your classroom. Older students will more likely be with you for only a fifty-minute period, or an hour and a half if on the block system. In either case you must ensure that these thirty students with widely different emotional needs, behavioral tendencies, and learning styles move from one work period to another with minimum disruption and make maximum use of the time spent on each subject to learn it and develop some mastery around it. Each time you pause to help a struggling student, talking and laughter breaks out in another part of the room that you are not giving attention. Perhaps wads of paper or chewing gum begin flying around the other end of the room.

After frequent requests for cooperation, you begin to lose it and get into power struggles with those acting up most vocally. As your nerves fray, you finally do lose it. Unable to cope any longer, you order an offending student to the principal's office. Even if he dutifully goes, he is back in your classroom the next day, often acting up again. If this continues, he is singled out, given time outs, detentions, calls to his parent or guardian, and repeat trips to the office. Either this student learns to obey the authority of his teachers and principal or he is headed for suspension or transfer. Meanwhile, the 80 or 90 percent of your class who has better impulse control is absorbing a lesson of what happens to individuals who speak or act in defiance of the teacher's authority: don't talk back if you want to make it in the system.

We can all imagine this situation and empathize with the teachers who must do the best they can in these difficult environments. If they didn't address disruptive behavior, or find and address its underlying antecedents, they would be doing a disservice to the rest of the class. Teachers are increasingly held accountable to demonstrate through standardized testing that their students have learned the prescribed curriculum for that topic. But to effectively teach their students, they need to be able to get and keep their focused attention. This is why classroom management techniques are given such priority.

But what are these techniques?

As I have said, Jones grounds classroom management in an instructional system that appears to have great merit in equipping teachers to effectively help all thirty students in the class follow the lesson, at the same time building their confidence and skills. While doing so, he is simultaneously training teachers to maximize obedience to their every instruction, which is the part of his system I am focusing on. He begins with the arrangement of desks so that there are aisles and blocks of seats that permit the teacher to place herself next to any student with the minimal amount of steps possible. He has found that there is a "zone" of several feet in which students will more readily obey the teacher's instructions. We can immediately note that this fulfills one of Milgram's observations that physical proximity of the authority figure dramatically increases the rate of compliance.

He next takes meticulous pains to train teachers in the poise and bearing so that "no means no" and "arguing is not an option." The maxim he uses is that *"Any discipline management technique that is working should self-eliminate."* In other words, it should be so effective that the student internalizes it so completely that just being in the presence of the authority figure, or in the space "owned" by the authority figure even if that authority is physically absent, will trigger obedience to the authority's rules.

To achieve this, Jones trains teachers in the art of "meaning business." This means creating a presence so commanding and sending signals that are so clear that students do not dream of talking back or disobeying instructions. After constructively training teachers to control their own stress reactions to provocative student behavior, he develops their self-awareness of body language to a degree rivaling that of dancers, actors, and world class athletes.

Take this example. A teacher is bent over a student's desk for a few seconds to help the student with a lesson. A student across the room begins talking to another student in violation of the classroom rule to focus on one's own work and not talk to other students during individual work assignments. Jones acknowledges that the teacher will be torn between completing the instruction and reinforcing classroom discipline. He is unequivocal. Reinforcing discipline must always come first or the teacher will lose control of the entire class.

Therefore, Jones instructs teachers how to reinforce discipline by displaying they "mean business" in the most economical and effective way possible. He exhorts the teachers he is training to *"See and then act—don't think."* If they think, the values conflict between instruction and discipline will undermine the priority of classroom management.

Per Jones:

"When you set limits in the classroom, you are establishing behavioral boundaries for the students. You know from developmental psychology that children establish reality by testing boundaries. If the boundaries never change, testing extinguishes as the child accepts the limit as being part of his or her reality."

To reinforce the boundaries, Jones trains the teacher who is bent over a student's desk to immediately turn her attention to the noncompliant behavior on the other side of the room. The teacher shouldn't just turn any old way, but rather turn in a "regal fashion" that exudes "meaning business." There is an exact way to execute a slow regal turn, which Jones breaks into the component steps. They include:

"Excuse me" to the student you were giving instructional guidance.

Then take a full one second for each of the following steps:

One. Stay down and breathe gently.

Two. Straighten up halfway as you look toward the disruptive students.

Three. Finish straightening up while looking at the disruptive students.

Four. Slowly rotate your shoulders and waist toward the disruptive students.

Five. Point one foot toward the disruptive students as your hips come around.

Six. Bring your other foot around to complete the turn as you square up to the disruptive students.

Each of these steps is elaborated on for the power of their nonverbal language and is practiced in teacher training sessions. They are complemented by instructions on eye contact, hand placement, jaw position, and smile suppression. The image given to the teachers is that of the dour Queen Victoria coldly stating *"We are not amused."*

Surely, this is enough to send shivers down the spines of most children contemplating disobeying the classroom authority! It most closely resembles a rattlesnake unwinding for a strike!

The training Jones does is then imbedded in a carefully constructed system of rewards and penalties that further discourage any tendency to noncompliance with class rules and assignments.

Lee Canter's *Classroom Management for Academic Success* is even more focused on systems of rewards and penalties. Early in his book, Canter has a section on teaching behavior and borrows from Jones.

"Behaviors taught should include expectations regarding verbal behavior, movement, and participation. More than 90 percent of disruptive behavior is related to inappropriate student talking and

movement and lack of student participation in the activity before them (Jones 2000). Therefore, you need to specify the particular verbal behavior, level of movement, and participation you expect from students."[3]

I have no doubt whatsoever that Canter was or would be just as horrified as we are at the ordeal Louise Ogborn was put through. Nevertheless, I find the emphasis on controlling movement and speech eerily reminiscent of the deeply ingrained rule sets Louise was following when complying with the orders she was given.

Canter emphasizes the need for explicit directions. One example he gives:

Vague Directions

"I need everyone to pay attention."

Explicit Directions

"I need everyone's attention. That means your eyes are on me, there is nothing in your hands but your pencil, and no one is talking."[4]

If corrections officers are taught to be as exact in the instructions they give to inmates, and why wouldn't they be, then David Stewart ("Officer Scott") had his job made easier by teachers who had conditioned Louise Ogborn in exact compliance to explicit directions. Each time we go through airport security, we experience how exactly law enforcement authority is trained to issue explicit directions. Depending on the generation of technology in use, you may hear:

"Sir, remove everything from your pockets, remove your belt, remove your shoes, take the laptop out of its case."

"Ma'am you are not to touch anything while I check your bag."

All this is done apparently for a good cause, but is always dependent on our obedience and simultaneously reinforces our conditioning to obey.

Like Jones's book, Canter also provides many useful techniques to assist teachers in performing their jobs. I am not focusing on those because they are outside of our purpose of exploring the subjects of obedience and Intelligent Disobedience. I am focusing on how training a million and a half teachers in classroom management may have the unanticipated meta-effect of creating a climate of obedience that potentiates authority running amok.

Both classroom management systems include "back-up plans" or in Canter's terminology "consequences from a discipline hierarchy." For middle/secondary school he offers a sample plan.

First disruption:	*Warning*
Second disruption:	*Stay 1 minute after class*
Third disruption:	*Stay 2 minutes after class*
Fourth disruption:	*Call to parents*
Fifth disruption:	*Send to vice principal's office*

Again, there is nothing inherently wrong with this system, but it has the meta-effect of instilling a respect for/fear of increasing consequences for noncompliant behavior. Louise Ogborn "knew" if she did not comply that the consequences would escalate; in this case to being arrested and taken to jail.

Canter goes on to give explicit regimens on how to instruct students to behave in every aspect of classroom life from early education onward. Jones acknowledges the need for complete control of these common classroom activities as well, though provides more systemic guidelines. Here are some of the topics covered.

- Beginning-of-day routine
- End-of-day routine
- In-seat transitions (between activities)
- Out-of-seat transitions (between activities)
- Lining up to leave the classroom

- Walking in line
- Entering the classroom after recess or lunch
- Distributing and collecting materials and papers
- Sharpening pencils
- Using materials on bookshelves or cabinets
- Leaving class to go to the bathroom
- Taking care of desks, table, and chairs
- Using the drinking fountain[5]

Undoubtedly, these topics are being updated as students increasingly have access to electronic communications. Each of these may make perfect sense individually. Collectively and cumulatively, it is only reasonable to assume there are meta-effects. In fact, both of these classroom management systems count on that. If the behavioral management is sufficiently consistent, it becomes internalized self-management. The rule sets disappear from consciousness and become the default behavior. If the intended result is orderly classrooms, this may be desirable. It is not desirable if the meta-result is nurses, copilots, security personnel, or McDonald's hourly workers being obedient when they should not be.

If there are 180 school days in a year and students attend school for 13 years between kindergarten and high school, allowing for a few absences each year, students are in school approximately 2,300 days by the time they have completed high school. At a little over 6.5 hours a day in most schools, each of our children spend about 15,000 hours of their lives in some form of classroom management system before graduating high school. According to Malcolm Gladwell in his best-selling book, *Outliers: The Story of Success*, it takes about 10,000 hours of practice to become masterful at an activity. Have we designed a system that makes too many of our citizens masterfully obedient by the time they leave their secondary education? Or masterfully (but not intelligently) disobedient if they have learned to rebel against this system?

This is not to say that our current system of education is the cause of obedience to authority or to the misuses of authority. As I have noted, every culture has its means of inculcating respect for authority. To some degree, I venture to say that the elaborate systems for classroom management offered by Jones, Canter, and others is a response to past systems no longer being in favor. Prior generations were comfortable with teachers using corporal punishment and humiliation to enforce discipline. In other cultures, secondary education is not universal while at the same time being essential for economic security; this combination carries sufficient economic and social incentives to make classroom management a nonissue. In segments of societies without access to formal schooling of any kind, the genetic disposition toward obedience is still expressed and reinforced through a variety of social and religious norms and sanctions.

This book, and this chapter in particular, focuses on the universal primary and secondary education system found in most economically developed nations as a prime shaper of obedience to formal authority. There is no doubt that obedience to mother, father, or other primary caregivers laid the early foundation for obedience to future authority figures. Surely, religious education and extra-curricular activities with other authority figures reinforce the lessons learned. But none span the years of young human development for so long and so intensely in the developed world as classroom education.

Louise Ogborn was a product of that system. So were, for that matter, Donna Jean Summers and "Wes" Nix Jr. So were the victims and perpetrators in the seventy other establishments allegedly successfully targeted by David Stewart.

I am sure there are educators who can make profound critiques of the philosophy of education itself and offer radically alternative models that reduce the emphasis on authority. I would undoubtedly applaud some of these models. Perhaps the blending of virtual and physical classrooms that is beginning to occur through creative uses of technology will de-emphasize classroom authority as a byproduct of the new media and methodologies. But the current reality is that most of our education through secondary school occurs in classrooms to which tens of millions of children report daily. Some of the questions the stories presented above require us to ask include:

1. What can be done to retain that which is valuable in classroom management techniques while reducing their tendency to create unthinking obedience?

2. How do we train new teachers to develop a healthy autonomy in their students while maintaining order?

3. How do we retrain experienced teachers who have successful classroom management skills to encourage independent thinking?

4. When students transition from the school system and become frontline workers who have minimum job and financial security, how do we train them to question orders that violate safety, legality, or common decency?

5. How do we train frontline supervisors to clarify orders they receive and evaluate their safety, practicality, and legality before acting on them?

6. How do we develop healthy relationships between children and those in authority that form a foundation for both classroom and workplace behaviors?

We will begin to answer these questions in the next chapter.

Chapter Ten

Teaching Intelligent Disobedience: Where Do the Lessons Begin?

W E ARE LEFT WITH THE CLEAR SENSE that there are many benefits to teaching Intelligent Disobedience in human development. How to do so appears to have been given little attention in the formal education stages of that development. Both research and application are scarce. Nevertheless, the subject is important enough for us to begin pulling together elements from different sources that could be used in laying early groundwork for Intelligent Disobedience competence.

As far back as his 1985 commencement speech at Stanford, President Donald Kennedy talked about authority in education. He observed the following:

> *"We are reminded of one fascinating aspect of guide dog training called 'intelligent disobedience.' The dogs must learn to resist the master's authority, but only when they see something is wrong (a speeding car, a hole in the path). So it must be with education in a democratic society; students must learn as an essential part of their education how and when to resist and challenge aspects of that very education. The idea of selective, intelligent disobedience to educational authority should, we think, be favored as an educational aim."*

Unfortunately, it has not been favored. Huge amount of resources are spent on finding the best ways to help students succeed, to improve standardized test results, and in more humanistic settings to develop social skills, self-esteem, creativity, and resiliency. But we are hard pressed to find mentions of Intelligent Disobedience by that or any other name. As we have seen, it is often quite the contrary.

An exception in the literature is an article by David Nyberg and Paul Farber titled "Authority in Education." The authors, fully appreciating the importance of teaching healthy relationships to authority, observe a paradox in the very structure of the teacher-student relationship.

> *This question of how one shall stand in relation to authority is the foundation of educated citizenship: Its importance cannot be overemphasized. Teachers, we believe, have a special obligation to teach about authority while they act as authorities in supervising education.*[1]

Consider what skill this requires on the part of the teacher! We have seen the stresses many classroom teachers experience. What training and self-management are required to exercise the legitimate authority of the teacher's role while inculcating a meta-message about the appropriate limits of authority?

It is true that the best teaching programs emphasize the development of critical-thinking skills on the part of students. But do those programs sufficiently prepare teachers to use challenges to their own authority as practice opportunities for students to productively develop independent judgment in the face of authority? It is one thing to think critically; it is another to express the outcomes of that thinking when it challenges positional authority and still another to act on those outcomes. Developing critical thinking without simultaneously developing the attitudes and competencies to express and act on that thinking is not adequate preparation for corporate or political citizenship. When we look at the 2014 website of the Center for Critical Thinking at Sonoma State University (www.criticalthinking.org), we see a wonderfully complete set of materials for training teachers to teach critical thinking at every level of education, but we do not see a single item regarding translating critical thinking into appropriate resistance to the flawed policies or orders that emanate from authority.

If we go back to The Seeing Eye, Inc., we are now talking about the role being played by Dave Johnson, director of training. Dave is not just responsible for the training of guide dogs in Intelligent Disobedience; Dave must first train the trainers who train both the dogs and their handlers. We have seen how precise the methodology is in order to help the guide dogs learn the distinction between when to obey and when to disobey. Failure to be fully consistent results in loss of confidence in the dog and in its handler. How much practice is needed for classroom teachers to consistently create the conditions that support the confident development of Intelligent Disobedience? We saw the detailed level of indoctrination and practice that goes into many classroom management programs. How much Intelligent Disobedience training do teachers need to create an appropriate balance? We don't know because it doesn't appear to have been tried.

Authors Nyberg and Farber, in turn, cite foundational work on authority and education by Kenneth Benne. Benne's conceptual constructs are challenging, but he sums up the educational task well in a memorable line, though it may help us if we mentally replace his invented word, anthropogogy (by which he means all stages of human development), with the more common word, pedagogy.

All anthropogogy is at once a mothering and a weaning, a rooting into ongoing authority relations and a pulling up of roots.[2]

What a vivid image: rooting our young in appropriate respect for authority and whatever cultural and topical wisdom it can transmit, then helping them break sufficiently free of that authority to establish their own sense of how to be in and contribute to the world.

How do we do this effectively? How do educators simultaneously instill those being educated with the knowledge and respect of authority and the discernment to know when to think differently than that authority, even to resist it and act counter to it? To exert the equivalent of the intelligent guide dog's counter-pull?

Benne observes:

> Teachers were taught first to establish order in the classroom and then to proceed to the business of teaching students what, it was assumed, they needed to learn.... It is a quite novel practice for most educators— teachers, parents, or administrators—to seek to utilize conflict openly and responsibly as a way toward learning for themselves and for those with whom they find themselves in conflict.[3]

We might ask, why is this approach so novel among teachers, parents, and administrators? This is probably a more important question than it may seem to be. If teachers are to effectively encourage students to question authority, they must themselves embody the experience of effectively questioning authority. The administrators to whom they report are already a harried breed. They struggle to balance the educational requirements of the state; interest groups representing students with special needs; teachers' unions; parent groups; individual parents; fluctuations in population relative to school infrastructure, transportation, and lunchroom needs; health and safety programs; language and cultural diversity; rapidly changing technology; perennial budget constraints; and a host of other matters. Are they really prepared to value their faculty questioning their own authority?

Until those in positions of authority in any environment experience the value of Intelligent Disobedience at saving them from painful mistakes, of finding better ways to achieve the goals for which they are responsible, it is hard to give more than lip service to the idea. Initiatives to create cultures that support Intelligent Disobedience at the level of a whole school system, or even of a single school, need to begin thoughtfully in order to honor and transform the natural resistance that will occur.

This is not to say that changes in teacher training programs to create a balance to existing classroom management techniques can't be tested simultaneously. Relatively simple exercises can be included that develop the confidence and skills needed to encourage productive conflict without fear of losing control of the classroom. Perhaps this is too much to ask of newly minted educators. Perhaps it needs to be sequenced into ongoing professional development. Nevertheless, it is clearly a critical capability if we are to lay the foundations for independent thinking, responsible citizenship, and Intelligent Disobedience.

But is teacher training even the place to start? What about the earliest patterns of obedience learned in home life? Are they creating sufficient distinctions in the minds of our young about when to obey and when to question before obeying?

Aristotle, who wrote at length on education, noted this:

The things which we are to do when we have learnt them, we learn by doing them; we become for instance good builders by building and good lyre players by playing the lyre. In the same way it is by doing just acts that we become just, by doing temperate acts that we become temperate, by doing brave deeds that we become brave. . . . It is of no little importance, then, that we should be habituated this way or that from the earliest youth; it is of great importance or rather all-important.[4]

Sharon Presley, a libertarian social psychologist who specializes in obedience and resistance to authority, in an article titled "Not Everyone Obeys: Personal Factors Correlated with Resistance to Unjust Authority," laments,

Unfortunately, few, if any, programs are going to teach children to be critical of authority and the law. Parents are on their own with teaching that attitude.[5]

As we have seen, she is woefully correct. Yet, given Aristotle's admonition, how do parents lay the groundwork for Intelligent Disobedience?

We know the incredible plasticity of young minds; for example, their ability to absorb the content and patterns of language. We can see the virtue in early exposure to what is appropriate and inappropriate obedience. But surely we cannot cede authority to a five year old without adverse consequences. Nyberg and Farber show us this is a false choice. We do not need to cede authority in order to help children develop an appropriate relationship to it. They note:

> Parents and educators can help teach this capacity by increasingly encouraging questions about the why and wherefore of their own requests for obedience and agreement.[6]

After a parent gives a child direction, she might ask:

> *"Why do you think I am telling you to do that?"*
> *"What do you think might happen if we don't do that?"*
> *"Can you think of another way for us to _____?"*

Nyberg and Farber go on to say:

> Responding to these questions with reasons will gradually replace subjection with understanding in the young.[7]

Clearly, the use of the stereotypical, "Because I said so" does not pass this test. You can think of a range of responses based on the situation that could pass the test, such as:

> "We need to do this because we gave our word that we would. Keeping our word is one of the values of this family."

> "We need to do this because it is safer than not doing it. One of my jobs as a parent is keeping the family safe."

> "We need to clean up the table because other people will sit here after us and would appreciate having a clean place to eat."

> "This is an emergency so I don't have time to explain to you why we are doing this, but I will explain after the emergency is taken care of."

Easy for me to say, isn't it? I'm not in the restaurant with the child throwing pasta on the floor or in the grocery store pulling packs of chewing gum off the shelves. The trick is to consistently give clear, age-appropriate reasons the child can understand, despite the pressures of life you are under. To do this takes a commitment to self-management. It may well require breaking the patterns of exercising authority we were exposed to when we were children. The bias to creating obedience is insidious. But with self-awareness and commitment, we can fulfill the parental and societal role of transmitting the norms of the culture that must be followed without creating early patterns of blindly submitting to authority out of coercion, fear, or habit.

Contrast this to the benign, but nevertheless cautionary, tale told to me by a parent who is very active in her children's school system. She volunteers, among other things, in her city's middle school "Clothes Closet." The clothes are donated by families who no longer are using items that are still in good condition. They are made available to students whose families struggle to provide them with the variety of items needed in their rapidly growing early teens, especially in a city with a four-season climate. The donations are supplemented with other necessities, such as toiletries that may be difficult for the families to provide.

A student came to the Tuesday "shopper buddy program," which can take a degree of courage in the tough world of middle-school social dynamics. The volunteers asked the young girl what clothes and toiletry items she needed. Her response should send shivers of warning up our spines.

"Oh, I just do what adults tell me to do. That's what my parents say to do. So you can just tell me what I need."

Once again, we see loving parents trying to take care of their children and, inadvertently, creating behavioral programming for compliance that is then reinforced by the rest of society's socialization mechanisms.

One educator made the observation that parents instilling respect for, and fear of, authority may be more prevalent among the disadvantaged segments of society. The adults in the household often have personally experienced the power of authorities to control their fate, or those of family members and neighbors, in employment, social services, law enforcement, and the judicial, prison, and probation systems. The penalties for nonconformity and disobedience can be high, indeed.

Even the Clothes Closet volunteer, very securely in the middle class, reflected on how she might be instilling a value system that unintentionally could be predisposing her children to misplaced obedience. She writes:

> *"I turn to my own parenting skills and exactly what I am teaching my kids at times. In the interest of blindly having them show their 'nice skills' (meaning their socially polite skills), I'm certain that sometimes they have received the message 'to be kind over using your intuitive skills.'"*

She is hitting the problem nail squarely on the head. Let's see what else we can learn to create the balance we are seeking.

What We Are Teaching

What is it exactly that we should be trying to teach our children at home or in school about obedience? Milgram gives us a clue as he tries to make sense of what his experiments reveal. He does not suggest to us how to go about it, but his analysis does shine light on the powerful mechanisms at work.

Milgram sees human beings as capable of existing in two distinct states. One is a *state of autonomy* in which we make choices based on our own understanding of what is right and wrong. The other is in a state of hierarchical relationships in which we become the agent of those at higher levels. He calls this an *agentic state*, meaning we are acting as an agent on behalf of an authority's judgments and instructions, rather than on our own.

This agentic state has permitted civilizations to create complex systems that are capable of achievements on a grand scale. They make large nation-states, in which we live, possible. By thousands of people implementing the instructions of various authorities, we have developed the infrastructure for global commerce, made it possible to send human beings to the moon, and in its darker manifestations, to wage large-scale wars of conquest and destruction.

Milgram observes that once a human being shifts from the autonomous state to the agentic state, it is difficult for most to easily shift back. He posits that doing so would be a repudiation of the system that is supporting his identity and survival. Yet, remaining only in the agentic state where the individual does not feel responsible for his actions because they are not originating with him is, as we know, highly dangerous.

If we accept Milgram's analysis, then the answer to the question *What are we trying to teach our children at home and in school about obedience?* is the nature of these two states, how they come about, what they feel like, and the capacity for shifting between them when it is appropriate to do so.

It would seem that we need to devise pedagogical programs using age-appropriate methods for doing several things:

1. Creating an understanding of the two states and their function

    Sometimes people do things they decide to do, and sometimes they do things others have told them they need to do.

    What are examples of things "the person decides to do," and what are examples of "they do what they are told"?

2. Creating awareness of the two states within the experience of those being educated

    In your own life, when do you do things you decide?

    When do you do things others tell you to do?

3. Creating awareness of how to self-regulate the tendencies of each state

When you decide what to do, what are the kinds of things you need to think about? (Is it safe, fair, enjoyable, hurtful to others, best way, and so forth?)

When you do what others tell you to do, what are the kinds of things you need to think about? (Who is telling you? Does he or she have the right to tell you? Is what he or she is telling you to do harmful? And so forth.)

4. Creating awareness of when to let either state be dominant

Under what conditions is it better to do what others are telling you to do?

Under what conditions is it better to question or resist what you are being told to do, even if it seems hard to refuse?

5. Creating a bridge between the states that preserves personal accountability, despite acting as an agent

When you do what you are told, why are you still responsible for what you do?

Are you always still responsible?

6. Developing the language and skills to translate that sense of accountability into speech and action

If you are not comfortable doing what you are told, how do you say so?

How do you resist doing something even when you are pressured to do it?

Clearly, there are whole books to be written, and curricula to develop and test, on how to do this well and imaginatively. At what stage is it appropriate to begin this training? Some may argue that we cannot teach these levels of distinction at too young an age, and surely there is merit to that position. They might use my own guide dog metaphor to make this point—guide dogs are not schooled in Intelligent Disobedience until they are about sixteen months old. If we use the common human-to-dog-year ratio, the child would be about nine or ten years old before these lessons begin.

Intelligent Disobedience and Childhood Safety

Sadly, we cannot wait until age nine or ten to begin laying the foundation for Intelligent Disobedience in humans. I regret that my research into the question of how we teach children to resist the inappropriate use of authority led me to the one area in our culture that is giving this question attention: the movement to prevent childhood sexual abuse.

Remember that Dave Johnson, The Seeing Eye director of training, first made the connection between teaching guide dogs Intelligent Disobedience and conveying these principles to his son, when his son was about to go off to camp for three weeks. The prospect of trusted adults, counselors, coaches or others betraying that trust generated significant concern for Dave and his wife. We know from painful experience in our society that such fears are far from unfounded in too many circumstances.

As a result, a body of practice has been developed with some urgency to teach children of all ages their autonomous rights and how to protect them despite being in a hierarchical setting in which they have appropriately ceded certain autonomy to legitimate authorities. What are some of the common elements of this early childhood training as it currently exists?

Boundaries

A starting point is the subject of boundaries. What is a boundary in human interaction? First and foremost, it is knowing that there is a distinction between you and others. The difference is most concrete in your body and in your right to be touched only in ways that are appropriate. As obvious as the distinction may sound, naming it and giving it validity create a foundation on which later distinctions between self and authority can be built.

Saying No

Another central goal is teaching the child when it is appropriate to say "no" and how to say it effectively. There are many ways in which "no" can be said ineffectively, such as shyly or while giggling or by failing to repeat it if the "no" is not respected. Here we are into the realm of "voice" that we examined earlier. These programs have children practice being aware of their body language, their eye contact, the strength of their statement, and different ways to repeat and command respect for the boundary they are setting.

Telling

A third is telling someone else. It is recognized that a solitary stand against abuses of authority is both difficult and dangerous. The abuser can threaten additional consequences for speaking of the abuse. Creating awareness of the need to get support as early as possible is another habit that can be taught and practiced that will serve well in both current and future situations.

Rejecting the Act

Some programs emphasize the distinction between saying no to a specific act and recognizing that does not necessarily mean rejecting the other person entirely. This is an important distinction. For example, in the case of an inappropriate boundary infringement by an adult family member, it may seem unthinkable to reject the family member, but the child can still firmly reject the act that makes him or her uncomfortable. Once again, this is a helpful foundation for building the capacity to take firm stands later in life toward those with whom one may need to live and work.

Look at this application by the son of parents who are deeply involved in the KidSafe Foundaiton, a nonprofit organization dedicated to preventing child abuse. Their son was clearly prepared to deal with a questionable situation in ways many young people are not.

> *We want him (our son) to be polite but NEVER at the expense of his safety and just because an adult, like a teacher or counselor, tells him to do something. If it makes him uncomfortable or confused, guess what? He doesn't have to do it! He has the right to say "NO" and he knows it. Blind obedience versus knowing when and how to be assertive is on my mind as my son tells me this experience he had at camp.*
>
> *My son is at a new camp. The first two days when changing for swim they changed in a huge bathroom that had stalls. My son (as did the other boys) went into their individual stalls and changed. The third day they were brought to a smaller bathroom (no clue why) and there were no stalls. My son said to the counselor, "I want to change in the stall." The counselor said, "We are in a rush, just change here, hurry up." My son responded, "I don't want anyone to see me and I don't want to see anyone else's privates." . . . The counselor raised his voice and told him he had to change. He refused. The counselor got the Director of the camp, who amazingly told my son, "I absolutely respect your right to privacy and you don't ever have to change in that bathroom again—you can always go to the big bathroom."[8]*

On an immediate basis, the training this child had been given equipped him to deal with an uncomfortable situation, regardless of whether it contained actual danger. More fundamentally, it switched the locus of his orientation from Milgram's "agentic state" to his own "autonomous state." As Aristotle observed, we learn to do things by doing them. We can project that this child will grow up better equipped to effectively move between these states as an adult. If this preparation were multiplied by millions of young people, it could advance the state of ethical behavior in group settings in ways that have eluded humanity throughout its history.

Such outcomes require determined and consistent inputs from adults who share responsibility for the young individual's character development. They will not arise from a lecture to children or a "talk" the night before they are first going to school or camp or to a church youth group or scout meeting. Ideally, modeling by adults will be reinforced by well-designed programs to create awareness, provide practice, and build confidence, much like the care we take developing Intelligent Disobedience in guide dogs.

Refusal Skills

Another child development educator offers this insight in an article entitled "Teaching Children Refusal Skills." This is a relatively new concept in our developmental culture. It seems to me that refusal skills are the toolbox of Intelligent Disobedience.

> *Children who are taught refusal skills are more likely to make positive choices and refrain from engaging in high-risk behaviors. Helping children set limits for themselves and say "no" to outside pressures increases their self-confidence. When children learn to stop and consider the consequences before responding to a request, as well as a variety of ways to say "no," they become more accomplished at refusing to participate in anything that could harm themselves or others.*[9]

The article contains many exercises and role plays to develop awareness and skills. In the role plays, it has the teacher pretend to be a peer who is trying to get the student to do something against his or her own good sense. This is clearly a step in the right direction in teaching appropriate resistance. But none of the role plays are designed to have the student practice when the teacher is the authority figure. This is a serious omission if we are to truly prepare individuals for Intelligent Disobedience. It is not, however, a great step from here to there in terms of designing role plays that do that.

Where should these exercises in developing the awareness and skills for appropriate resistance for Intelligent Disobedience be done? For the answer to this question, we can rely on our autonomous good sense or, somewhat ironically, turn again to the words of an authority, Kenneth Benne, whom we introduced earlier in this chapter:

> *Schools are only one among many socializing agencies that work to shape the minds and characters, the habits, outlooks, and modes of thinking of young people in today's societies, including our own. Recreation groups, mass media, churches, various peer-led youthful coteries, and conclaves are only a few of the agencies that, taken together, are more powerful than schools in current processes of enculturation and, as I would use the term, the education of youth.*[10]

If anything, this prescient observation is more true today, with the tremendous diversity of physical and virtual meeting places and activities. Yes, it could become tedious and formulaic to design and use training exercises for each of these activities; they would lose their power, much as the traditional safety briefing before an airplane takes off has lost its power. Nevertheless, a core program could be creatively adapted to different developmental ages and further contextualized for different settings. Nor do they necessarily need to be tedious, as the air travel industry has recently discovered by using hip, creative adaptations of the traditional message that still meet Federal Aviation Administration rules.

Here is an example given in a religious education context. I quote it at some length. What is particularly germane about this example is that it directly uses guide dog training as the metaphor to introduce Intelligent Disobedience to very young children. Although in this case the "voice within" the teacher refers to is characterized in religious terms, it can also be thought of in terms of the autonomous state Milgram describes. As in the case of the preacher who refused to go on in Milgram's experiment, we are not as concerned with how he conceptualized an alternative higher authority as we are that he could access a balancing locus to the experimenter's external authority.

I watched in amazement, as the term "Intelligent Disobedience" was demonstrated in flesh and blood by a blind woman and her dog.

During my first meeting of the Southeastern Guide Dog Georgia puppy raisers group, a blind woman told her dog to "Find the steps, Ralph." The large, white standard poodle quickly led the owner to the church auditorium stage steps.

"Forward up." Then "Left, left, Ralph." Up the seven steps they climbed and to the middle of the stage they walked.

"Right about, Ralph." They faced us, their audience, below.

She commanded her dog, "Forward, Ralph." The dog took a few steps forward, then stopped dead in its tracks.

"Forward, Ralph," she commanded again, with an impatient, stronger tone.

Ralph sat down five feet from the edge of the elevated stage. To follow its owner's order would have been easy for the dog—a quick jump. But it would have caused the blind woman to fall off the edge.

The Guide Dog overrode the "Forward" command with a greater "inner" command to protect its unsighted human. Right before my eyes, I saw why Intelligent Disobedience makes Guide Dogs top-of-the-line in trained canines. I was stunned and sold on becoming a volunteer puppy raiser!

Two months later, I picked up my very own future Intelligent Disobeyer from Southeastern Guide Dogs in Palmetto, Florida. Calypso, an 11-week old, black goldador, joined my First Day School (Sunday School in Quaker terminology) class of kindergartners, first- and second-graders. There were many lessons to be learned around Guide Dogs. Service, good manners, and being respectful of all of God's creatures were among such themes. . . . But teaching a class on "Intelligent Disobedience" seemed too Quakerly, too First-Day-Schooly, to pass up.

The youngsters sat quietly in their circle while I told the story with paper dolls of the visually impaired woman and her poodle. They, like me, were amazed the dog knew not to listen! He saved her from harm! How could a dog be so smart?

"This is called 'Intelligent Disobedience.' What is 'intelligent'?"

A second grader answered, "Smart."

Yes!

"What is 'disobedience'?

The answer took longer to bubble up. "Obey" they understood. Then "disobey" "Did the dog disobey?" "Have you ever disobeyed?" (Some of our children have never disobeyed! An amazing group of youths, indeed!)

And then the thorniest of questions, "Is it ever smart to disobey?"

NOOoooooo!! Thinking of mom or dad or teacher . . . right-o.

"Did the dog disobey?"

Well . . . yes . . . but still. . . . Those wheels were turning in those bright little minds!

"What if a stranger said, 'Come into my car.' " Wheels turning, turning, turning.

"Would you ever get into a car with someone you didn't know? By yourself?"

"NO!" quickly, emphatically, by one, then by all!

A classmate at school may ask you to cheat. You may want to lie about something that you know is wrong. The older you get, there will be more and more times you'll have to decide what to do. How will you know?

What will you do?

Aha! Your own smart brain! A small still Voice in your heart! The more you listen to that Voice, to that God Within, the more you will learn what the right thing to do is.

You need to practice listening to your small, still voice. Calypso needs to practice, too, so he will know what to do.

You children and our friend, Calypso, the Guide Dog, will learn to make the right decisions. He will learn Intelligent Disobedience. You will, too![11]

Is this teaching parable sufficient to create the capacity for Intelligent Disobedience? Perhaps for a few it may be. Sometimes lessons make a deep impact on the young. I think of the young girl who was in Thailand with her family when the great tsunami of December 2004 occurred the day after Christmas, killing a quarter of a million people. When the sea suddenly disappeared from the shore, hundreds of vacationers on a particular beach stared in astonishment or walked farther onto the now exposed seabed. This young girl remembered a lesson she had learned in school that the suddenly receding sea was the phenomenon that occurs before the sea comes crashing back in with the full force of a tsunami. She told her parents and had the family run as fast as they could away from the shore, saving her family's life from near certain death. The ultimate counter-pull.

In most cases, however, especially when authority is involved, it will take more than a teaching story to equip the student to take a stand against poorly thought out or harmful orders. A degree of practice will be needed to build the neural networks, the language patterns, the muscle memory, and the capacity to override emotional and social inhibitions.

Role Plays

This is where the methodologies of role play and improvisational theatre can be both powerful and engaging. In essence, this is how guide dogs and airline crews are trained in situational awareness, Intelligent Disobedience, and assertive voice or action.

It's also how we teach young children survival skills in the unlikely, but potentially catastrophic event of their clothes catching on fire. "Stop, drop, and roll." I recall a birthday party for my three-year-old daughter that we held at the local firehouse. The fee for using the upstairs communal space was left up to us as a contribution, but the agreement included that a segment of the party would be facilitated by a fire department officer conducting an exercise in stop, drop, and roll to extinguish flames. Try to picture twenty three-year-old children rolling on the floor, while my wife rolled her eyes at my concept of what a kids' birthday party should include. But I bet those kids remember those skills to this day should they be needed.

Face-to-face and virtual programs for developing the skills of Intelligent Disobedience in children will be developed, offered, taught, and supplanted by new programs over time. One such program as of this writing is the Search Institute whose motto is *"Discovering what kids need to succeed."* They have identified forty "assets" that equip a child for success. Twenty of these are external, provided by the people and systems in which the child is developing, and twenty are internal, there for the child to develop and tap. These vary by developmental age broken down into three to five year olds, five to nine year olds, eight to twelve year olds, and twelve to eighteen year olds.

The assets are developed and used in combination. One of these assets is resistance skills. Clearly, if it were used in isolation, we would be developing a pretty unbalanced individual, just as teaching a guide dog only disobedience would deprive the activity of value. So resistance skills are taught in combination with other assets such as responsibility, restraint, interpersonal competence, peaceful conflict resolution, and personal power. But the salient point for our purposes is that they are taught, and not just in relation to peers but also in relation to authority figures.

For example, in one of the books published by Search Institute, there is the following exercise titled "Police Encounter: Dealing with Authorities." It sets the scene for the skit as follows:

A teenager comes home with her friends at night and doesn't have a key. Her parents aren't home so she climbs in through a window and

*lets her friends in. As there have been robberies in the neighborhood,
police have been doing extra patrols, notice unusual behavior and
come to the house to check it out. When the teen answers the door
the police officer wants to know what she and her friends are doing
in the house. The officer doesn't believe she lives there and starts
asking a lot of questions.*[12]

The skit calls for variations. In one, the police officer is being courteous. In another variation, the police officer is being intimidating and accusatory. The role players are asked to use their skills to deal with the situation, including resistance skills so they remain courteous yet firm about their right to be there, even when under pressure.

This is an age-appropriate scenario for building the competency to productively stand up to authority, despite both its symbolic and real power. It can be run through several times with different teens playing the role of the one who lives there and with different "officers" presenting varying styles of wielding authority. The role plays can then be debriefed. What were the choices for the teen in that situation? What emotions did they experience in the face of the different styles of authority? How well did they use the elements of voice, body language, self-regulation, and persistence to establish their right to be there? What might they do differently or better if they encounter similar situations in life?

How effectively do such role plays actually change behavior? We have hard evidence of this in guide dog training and airline crew training. It is an area that would benefit greatly from controlled studies of different approaches in different situations and at different stages of development.

Unfortunately, the cautionary note in the introduction to this book must be repeated here when adapting this role play to the needs of boys and young men of color. As their parents know all too well, their survival may depend on complete outward obedience when stopped and questioned by police. This is an example of how developmental activities will need to be tailored to the needs of cultures and subcultures so they do more good than harm. In the case of minorities facing disproportionate stop-and-search procedures, it may be even more urgent to provide Intelligent Disobedience training with specific skills for avoiding dangerous retaliatory responses by the authority.

While we look to the future to study the effectiveness of different approaches, we can surmise how even a small amount of this type of training may have been enough to equip Louise Ogborn to exercise Intelligent Disobedience that terrible evening at the McDonald's restaurant. She told her interviewer that as she obeyed Nix's increasingly humiliating instructions,

"I just went numb to everything so I could just survive."

Clinical psychologist Jeff Gardira observed about Louise's strategy,

"It's almost an out-of-body existence. It's like they're standing right next to themselves and they can't do a thing about it."

Maybe, with a little prior practice, Louise and the victims of this authority imposter in seventy other locations could have overridden the thrall that even pseudo-authority figures can hold over people and effectively resisted the orders that should not have been obeyed.

Principles of Teaching Intelligent Disobedience

Whether you are a parent, a teacher, an ethicist, or a concerned citizen reading this, you know that introducing this type of curriculum into the mainstream school system will be an uphill battle in most places. There are too many demands on our school systems and too many philosophies of what must be given priority.

Therefore, the way the culture will most effectively change is if readers like you find ways of introducing even small doses of

Intelligent Disobedience practice into your circles of activity. Those include any of the youth character and skill formation activities with which you may be involved: organized sports, religious education, boys and girls outdoor programs, self-defense training, community service, big brother and big sister relationships, summer camp, online safety instruction, and more. There are many opportunities for meaningfully laying the foundations of distinguishing appropriate obedience from inappropriate obedience, as well as the skills for doing right when told to do wrong.

Let me try to distill a few principles we gather from this chapter that can assist your efforts. Remember, though, I am the authority figure in this book, which leaves you responsible for determining if the lessons I am drawing seem the correct and important ones.

1. We are seeking appropriate ways of instilling the attitudes and skills of Intelligent Disobedience from the earliest meaningful developmental age at which this can be done.

2. Teaching is most often done by those in a relationship of authority toward those being taught, requiring consciousness by the teacher of the responsibility to balance the use of that authority with the invitation to appropriately question it.

3. Our goal is to make individuals aware that even when they are acting according to the dictates of authority, they are responsible for the choice to execute the dictates or not, based on the beneficial or harmful impact their choices will have.

4. In the home, we have the opportunity from preschool age onward to instill the habits of intelligent obedience by offering explanations and asking questions that engage a child as to why an action is or is not appropriate to take.

5. We are developing in children a conscious awareness of the legitimacy of requests by authority and the legitimacy of their

own moral sense, as well as how to reconcile the two when they are not in alignment.

6. In formal learning settings like schools or organized youth groups, teaching stories and demonstrations by trained guide dogs and handlers can produce memorable examples of appropriate obedience and disobedience.

7. We need to design age-appropriate and culture-appropriate role plays to practice the required skills of Intelligent Disobedience, presenting increasingly complex challenges to practice problem solving in unique situations.

8. By teaching children to respect their feelings of right and wrong in relation to their bodies, we are equipping them to fend off sexual abuse and laying a foundation for legitimizing their life-long right to autonomous choice.

9. At all levels of Intelligent Disobedience training, the elements of physical posture and voice need to be addressed so the resistance to harmful orders is made with sufficient assertiveness yet is culturally appropriate.

10. Whatever methods and frequency we select, we must intentionally balance the implicit cultural training for obedience with the explicit skills needed to disobey when self-protection, human decency, and responsible citizenship require doing so.

CHAPTER ELEVEN

Doing Right at Work: Saving Lives and Accomplishing Missions

FOR THOSE OF YOU WHO began to read this book for its application in the workplace, thank you for having taken this deep dive with me into the roots of inappropriate obedience in childhood development. For those of you who are reading this book for its application to childhood development, I invite you to join me once again in looking at the benefits of Intelligent Disobedience in the workplace, where the children being raised will soon find themselves.

Ideally, developing the good citizenship skill of Intelligent Disobedience is made easier when the groundwork is laid in childhood education. Meanwhile, we are left to live and work in a world in which the pressures to conform and obey are powerful. We need to decide how we will equip ourselves to resist ill-conceived or dangerous orders and how we will create environments that support Intelligent Disobedience for those in our care.

Preparation is a critical factor, for it may be too late to develop the discipline at the moment it is most needed. Let's examine the most memorable event that ushered in the twenty-first century as an example of this.

On the morning of September 11, 2001, Cyril Richard "Rick" Rescorla was on the job as a vice president for security at Morgan Stanley Dean Witter, which had some 3,700 employees in the World Trade Center, including 2,700 in the south tower. By a coincidence only of note to this book, Rescorla lived in Morristown, New Jersey, where The Seeing Eye is located. That morning, as he did every weekday morning, Rescorla drove to the Morristown station and waited for the 6:00 a.m. train on the same platform used to train seeing eye dogs in Intelligent Disobedience.

Rescorla had come to Dean Witter years earlier, prior to its acquisition by Morgan Stanley, to head up its security operation. A professional who was unusually alert to systemic danger, Rescorla, with the help of a former military colleague, quickly appraised the danger of terrorist attack to the twin towers. The towers, the tallest buildings in the world at that time, were symbols of Western culture, which was under attack by radical Middle East groups that had perpetrated a number of serious bombing attacks over the previous few years. The towers were particularly vulnerable due to their structural overreliance on internal supporting columns. Rescorla and his colleague wrote a detailed assessment of the risks for the Port Authority of New York, who owned the buildings, giving remedial recommendations. These recommendations were dismissed as too costly and politically unpalatable.

In 1993, with Rescorla on duty, the towers were subject to a massive truck bomb attack in the underground garage, which caused significant damage and casualties. This event reinforced Rescorla's well-reasoned concerns about the vulnerability of the towers and the potential for being the target of subsequent, more lethal attack. He was not able to persuade Morgan Stanley executives to abandon their lease and move out of the buildings. But he did achieve support for his insistence on implementing evacuation drills at monthly intervals to prepare for such an attack. Knowing the cost of having 3,700 employees of a New York investment firm take time to do safety drills, this in itself is noteworthy. Reports indicate that he had to stand up to the pressure of high-powered executives who resented the intrusion on their and their staff's schedules. This was the prior act of Intelligent Disobedience that made his subsequent act on 9/11 awesomely effective.

When the first plane hit the north tower at 8:46 a.m. on the morning of September 11, 2001, Rescorla saw the tower burning from his office on the forty-fourth floor of the south tower. We can imagine the surge of adrenaline he experienced at that moment. Unlike many others who felt shock, panic, and confusion, Rescorla had a plan and had practiced it. So when the announcement from the Port Authority came over the public address *urging people to stay at their desks*, there was no hesitation on recognizing this was a directive to ignore and to counter emphatically. This was the quintessential act of Intelligent Disobedience performed without hesitation that saved thousands of lives.

Rescorla grabbed his bullhorn, walkie-talkie, and cell phone and began systematically ordering Morgan Stanley employees to evacuate the south tower and the adjacent World Trade Center 5 building. Due to his urging, they followed the drill with speed and orderliness. If we can extend our canine metaphor, Rescorla was now operating like an insistent sheepdog from his native Cornwall, England.

All but three of Morgan Stanley's employees escaped with their lives. That is a staggering achievement in the face of nearly two thousand lives lost in the towers that day. One who didn't survive was Rescorla, who went back into the building searching for any stranded employees. That last act was one of heroism, which has been honored appropriately with medals and public praise. But the great lessons of developing his own situational awareness of risk, of persuading the power structure of the organization to respond at least partially to that risk, of creating plans to mitigate the risk, of rehearsing those plans with thousands of people and employing informed and Intelligent Disobedience at the moment those plans needed urgent implementation have not received the full attention they deserve.

Three Pillars of Safety and Correct Violation

The success of Rescorla's actions rested on three pillars, described by Professor James Reason, whose work I am going to bring into this discussion. It focuses on safety in complex organizations, which is often the environment in which Intelligent Disobedience must be exercised. His analysis is not based on the events of the Morgan Stanley evacuation but captures them well.

There would appear to be three main elements: the identification and assessment of an expected hazard . . . the development, testing and training of a set of counter measures designed to neutralize the threat . . . and an effective and timely way of deploying these countermeasures, a process relying critically on situational awareness. The latter has three components: perceiving the critical elements in the current situation, understanding the significance of these elements, and making projections as to their future status.[1]

Clearly, all of these elements are found in guide dog behavior and training, in Crew Resource Management training, and in other preparations we have examined. What seems to be missing from Professor Reason's analysis, if it were applied to the situation that faced Rescorla, was the need for a fourth element of Intelligent Disobedience, both in developing and training the countermeasures to the potential hazard and in executing them at the required, traumatic moment.

In fact, though, Professor Reason's work covers this element using different language in his earlier description of the "12 varieties of rule-related behavior."[2] The aptly named Reason offers a comprehensive analysis of the permutations that can exist in a safety-related situation. These include compliance or noncompliance to appropriate rules or procedures, inappropriate rules and procedures, and situations not foreseen or covered by existing rules and procedures. He cautions about the dangers of slipping into habits of noncompliance to rules that serve an appropriate purpose. This is an important caution for us to bear in mind because it would not be Intelligent Disobedience to disregard those rules.[3] In contrast to this, he draws attention to another of the twelve potential responses, which he calls "correct violation." Given the context in which an event occurs, it may be foreseeable that following the usual rule would not work. In that context, Intelligent Disobedience is a correct violation.

Although dramatic events like Rescorla's responses to the events at the twin towers are useful to alert us to the life and death potential of Intelligent Disobedience, every day, in organizations of every type, smaller acts of Intelligent Disobedience can keep programs on the rails and personnel in rule-bound bureaucracies and earnings-driven corporations from taking actions that would bring harm to their customers or constituents and discredit to their organizations.

In earlier chapters we have examined a number of the skills needed for effective Intelligent Disobedience such as situational awareness, assertive voice, and seeking allies who will also resist destructive orders. There is an additional element that should be included in developing effective responses.

Timing and Social Interaction

This element is found in an important analysis of Milgram's experiments that we have not yet covered. It is the roles of timing and social interaction in determining an outcome of either misguided obedience or appropriate resistance.

Think back to the situation in which Betty Vinson, the mid-level WorldCom accountant, found herself. When she was first approached about manipulating the monthly report to hide the fact of corporate losses, Betty hesitated. She then allowed herself to be convinced to participate despite her discomfort at doing so. From there Betty found herself on a slippery slope. Each month, when a fresh request was made, she continued to go along until she was confronted by an internal auditor and could no longer contain the strain she felt about her participation in the malfeasance. By then it was too late. She had colluded in enough illegal activity to earn a jail sentence. Yet, she was so close to saying "no" early on. She had even written a letter of resignation, and then tore it up. The more she participated in the cover-up, the less able she was to extract herself from the web she helped weave.

Through a careful analysis of films that were taken of some of Milgram's experiments, researchers found that the earlier an individual began to clearly resist, the more likely he or she was to end up refusing to go on with the experiment.[4] This may sound self-evident, but there is an important dynamic occurring.

The subjects in the experiment, in almost all cases, experienced significant strain between wanting to cooperate with authority and not wanting to continue inflicting harm. They had a psychological contract to assist the researcher with the learning experiment. As they began to see the pain the experiment appeared to cause, the strain of whether they should continue, or refuse to continue, grew. The subject needed to resolve that strain, one way or another.

This analysis of the films found that subjects use a gradation of behaviors to respond to the strain:

- ◆ **Cooperation phase.** Initially subjects assist the experimenter and experience little strain.

- ◆ **Strain phase.** When they begin to experience psychological/ moral strain, participants try to resolve it by either checking with the experimenter as to whether what was happening was supposed to happen or by notifying the experimenter that the symptoms were getting worse. These are relatively passive ways of expressing the strain. They are hints at what the subject is experiencing, not assertive declarations. If they feel reassured by the experimenter's responses, this reduces the strain and they accede to the instructions to continue. If the strain persists, they move to the next phase.

- ◆ **Divergence phase.** In this phase, participants actively or overtly question what is occurring or clearly object to the impact the experiment is having. When the experimenter insists the experiment must continue, some comply to resolve the strain, rationalizing as to why they should (the experimenter is trained, it's not lethal, I'm just doing what I've been told, etc.). If they could not or would not rationalize their continued compliance, the strain persists and they move to the next phase.

- ◆ **Divergence reduction or amplification.** The subject can reduce divergence and resolve or compartmentalize the strain by submission to the insistence of the authority figure to continue the experiment. Or the subject can amplify divergence, drawing clear distinctions between his and the experimenter's values hierarchy, and state an unambiguous refusal to continue.

Interrupting the Mesmerizing Effect of Authority

What this research adds to our understanding of protocols for training in Intelligent Disobedience are at least three things:

First, the analysis of these behaviors in the Milgram films shows that the earlier a subject overtly questions or objects, the more likely he is to break off the experiment before its end. Those who wait longer to voice questions or objections are more likely to resolve the strain they experience by complying with the experimenter through to the end. The longer they comply with the orders, the more they must rationalize their participation and the less likely they are to break with the authority.

Second, we form an understanding that the strain of the values clash must be resolved and there are two paths for resolution: one of obedience and one of disobedience. In training human beings in Intelligent Disobedience, we will need to help them understand the inevitability of experiencing the discomfort of this strain, the need to be able to stand in that discomfort and make conscious choices about how to resolve that strain. In other words, the simple resolution of the strain through compliance is not sufficient.

Third, there is a mesmerizing flow that occurs when one begins to obey authority and can take on a life of its own. That flow can be, and needs to be, interrupted much like in martial arts when an attack needs to be slowed down or diverted using the opponent's own force. Voicing discomfort or asking for clarification of directions is insufficient to stop the flow. Direct questions or objections are more likely to interrupt the progression and expose the authority's inability to give satisfying answers to the points raised. The authority's inadequate or authoritarian response to resistance breaks the spell of authority and allows a recovery of one's own autonomy.

This sequence is at times observable in our own lives when we are faced with growing discomfort, not just about direct orders but about an activity in which we are involved—how the little league coach is berating players, how our minister is using the pulpit to advance distasteful views, how the boss is coming in increasingly late requiring us to cover for her. We can experience strain about whether to raise our voice concerning these matters, to interrupt them and possibly to change them. The longer we wait, the more intense the strain. Eventually, we resolve it by amplifying our divergence and saying something to the offender, or we rationalize that it is not appropriate to do so and we go along, perhaps compartmentalizing our discomfort. The longer we wait, the more likely it is we will go along.

Milgram marveled at the politeness of some subjects in the face of what they thought were harmful, even potentially lethal acts. We are social animals, and politeness serves us well in many situations. Sometimes we can effectively perform acts of Intelligent Disobedience politely but resolutely. We must also be able to act with determined impoliteness when necessary. In a dire situation, the sequence of breaking the spell of authority described previously may need to operate with only seconds between the stages.

While writing this chapter, I discussed these progressions and methods of preparing for an event, such as Reason's three pillars of safety or Crew Resource Management training, as well as the capacity to urgently respond to an actual event, with a group of my partner's family members. One of them had served in the navy as a submarine engineer. He shared a germane story of throwing politeness out the window, or we might say out the porthole if it had been a surface vessel.

The sub was on routine maneuvers and was preparing to surface. There are strict protocols, of course, to ensure the sub doesn't surface into harm's way. One of those maneuvers is to do a 360 degree sonar sweep at depth of 150 feet. Because sonar is usually detecting what is ahead of the vessel, the sweep is to detect anything that might be approaching the intended surfacing position from another direction. Nothing was reported.

The next maneuver is to do a 720 degree rotation of the periscope—twice checking the entire circle around the surfacing position. The officer of the deck conducted the sweep, saw nothing, and allowed the surfacing sequence to continue.

Neither of these sweeps proved to be competent.

By a stroke of good fortune, a young crew member, who was at the lowest rank on the vessel, requested "periscope liberty." In nautical terms that is a request for permission to perform a periscope sweep, to gain more operational experience. Permission was granted.

The seaman climbed into the periscope tower. As soon as he began his sweep, he saw the bow of a freighter coming straight toward the sub. Without the slightest "polite" or "mitigating" language, he barked out the command "Emergency deep!" That is the command that every crew member knew meant instantaneous execution of rapid dive sequence. In the aft of the vessel, the engineer who told this story, which was pieced together based on the subsequent After Action Review of the incident, received the extraordinary command for "full reverse" of the engines. Without knowing the context, he instantly complied and the vessel slowed its forward motion. The engineer knew from the simultaneous pitch of descent that the sub was in emergency dive mode. Seconds later he heard the unmistakable rumble of propellers pass overhead.

When the heart rate of everyone aboard began returning to normal, procedures were implemented to safely surface the vessel. An inspection of the hull revealed the antennae had been snapped off by the freighter's props. It could not have been a more narrowly avoided collision. The seaman who had overridden the officer's order to surface had clearly saved the ship from disaster and probably the careers of the officers of the vessel. Politeness would have been fatal. So would a lack of prior preparation.

At the same time, this story has value in reminding us of the importance of appropriate compliance. The engineer who received the command for full reverse of the engines complied instantly, per his training for dealing with emergencies. Being aft, he had no directly observable data of what was occurring to warrant the command; nor did he have any data that would lead him to question the command. His immediate compliance was as important to the safety of the vessel as the junior seaman's overriding a senior's order. This distinction, between appropriate and inappropriate obedience, is what makes either choice intelligent.

In the relatively slowed down time of much of the corporate or organizational world, we usually have hours or days to sort through the question of intelligent obedience or disobedience. Perhaps that makes the disciplines required of Intelligent Disobedience harder to perform, without the adrenaline rush that accompanies situations requiring instant response. This is all the more reason to make individual contributors and teams aware of the dynamics that work in favor of conformity and obedience and against Intelligent Disobedience.

Sooner or later, a boss is going to ask her subordinates to do something that shouldn't be done because she is missing information, the subordinates are misinterpreting the order, or the order is lacking in good judgment. Incorporating the fundamentals of Intelligent Disobedience into professional training will protect the whole organization from stepping in front of an oncoming car—or freight train.

There is a project management (PM) training company that teaches Intelligent Disobedience as a module it offers as part of its advanced level of PM training. The bane of all projects is mission creep, when the original scope of the project continues to be expanded without thought given to the impact on the timeline or the need for additional resources. Mission creep from customers is difficult enough to manage. When it is instigated by superiors, or superiors become advocates for the customer's expanding requirements, it is harder still to resist. Yet, every project manager knows that if the creep becomes a crawl and the crawl becomes a lurching zig-zag in direction, the chances of the project being successfully completed, or completed within budget, are greatly diminished. As the steward of the project, the PM has to be able to use all the tools of voice and resistance to shepherd it to completion.

Intelligent Disobedience can be taught freestanding, or it can be woven into other professional development. It is certainly a legitimate part of any ethics training. There are courses on "managing up," where this skill set is a natural fit. It can be incorporated into classes on leadership and followership, exploring what each owes the other. Clearly, safety training programs should create awareness and competency of the topic. High-level team building explores the need to avoid group think through maintaining one's own reality in the face of group pressure and is a natural stepping stone to individual accountability. Even a little Intelligent Disobedience training can reap outsized rewards.

Overcoming Barriers to the Organization's True Needs

It is common in organizational life for a positional leader to set a lofty goal or hold high expectations for performance, despite limited or reduced resources. Sometimes those goals or expectations are driven by the leader. Sometimes they are set for the leader by more senior leaders, by market analysts, by government programs, or by competitive necessity. Problems arise when there is so much pressure to achieve these goals that "anything goes." Witness WorldCom.

James Reason whose "pillars of successful actions" were all found in both Riscorla's and the submarine's successful preparation for and response to catastrophic failure, identifies *"the blinkered pursuit of the wrong kind of excellent . . . usually in the form of seeking to achieve specific performance targets"* as one of the three pathologies that make systems vulnerable to this failure.[5] We saw in the chapter on World-Com how widespread the obsession was with metrics and achieving targets.

In these cases, intelligent resistance may be needed, but almost always it is most successful if accompanied by offering alternative ways to achieve the underlying interest.

Let's say the boss wants to be able to report 100 percent safety for six months. To achieve this, he is discouraging reporting "minor" safety violations. I have seen this more than once. Perhaps you have seen or experienced similar pressure to "smooth" statistical reports.

Obeying would be decidedly unintelligent. Disobeying may simply result in being pushed aside for someone who will blindly obey. Coming back to the boss with a plan to aggressively find the root causes of each "minor" accident in order to reduce safety incidents to near zero is a potentially acceptable alternative. Especially if you point out that the "wrong kind of excellence" may come back to bite him, whereas the right kind of excellence is both the right thing to do and the professionally prudent course of action.

Equally common in organizational life is that the system itself may be generating the barriers to effective action, to ways forward through challenging obstacles. Almost anyone who works in a traditional organization shudders at the number of times they hear "we can't do that" in response to initiatives to improve some aspect of the organization's work. These obstacles may not take the form of a direct order, but rather in withholding of approval or help for taking reasonable actions to address legitimate needs. A proactive form of Intelligent Disobedience is needed.

Creative Intelligent Disobedience

In the private sector, if an innovative employee or team encounters too many obstacles to developing new products or methods, the more courageous ones go off and develop the breakthroughs outside of the company. The high-tech sector is full of such stories and of individuals who have become very rich as a result.

In the public sector, there are fewer options for leaving the system to develop alternative solutions to meet the needs of the constituencies being served. In the worst cases, this results in poor service and antiquated practices. In the best cases, this promotes the development of creative Intelligent Disobedience within the system.

Barry Richmond is a retired colonel in the Indiana National Guard. He is an avid student of leadership. We had the opportunity to share ideas and stories before a series of presentations I made at Franklin College, in Indiana. I asked him to elaborate on his stories, which are exemplary of creative Intelligent Disobedience.

In true form for a serious thinker on leadership, he mused as to:

> *"What is Intelligent Disobedience? Is it simply disobeying a direct problematic order? Or is it more fundamentally disobeying command intent? Or a particular interpretation of a regulation? Or, even more profoundly, is it disobeying the barriers we ourselves erect to discovering ways to do what is needed in a situation?"*

Richmond's story is a classic case of developing competence in overcoming barriers imposed by bureaucracies. The context of the story is the senior roles he held at key National Guard facilities in Indiana in the post-9/11 world. In that changed world, National Guard units played an increasingly critical part in the US response to militant extremism in the Middle East and adjacent regions. Resources were needed to support this enhanced mission. I have excerpted his remarks in the following paragraphs, choosing to leave them in his own, spirited voice.

The first NO.

There they sat in all their glory—used SUVs lined up in neat rows in the quartermaster lot of the Department of Natural Resources (DNR). I drove by them frequently and wondered what would become of them? We desperately needed some type of four-wheel vehicles in the Range Branch of the Camp I managed. If only . . . One day I asked a master sergeant to go to the DNR quartermaster and see what they were going to do with those vehicles. He told me they would be auctioned off to the highest bidder at their annual excess property auction. Mmm . . . Further discussion revealed that DNR could just transfer them to us since we fell under another state agency, the Military Department of Indiana. I was in hog heaven— now I could get enough vehicles for our range branch, as well as other directorates on the Installation. But first I had to endure my first learning experience of working through the bureaucracy of acquisition.

Initially it was "No, we cannot do that." I consulted some "can-doers" and researched the regulation. Answer: "Well maybe, but you have to do x and y and z and . . . by the way, there is no budget for any maintenance on the vehicles . . . so what are you going to do when they break down or need any maintenance?" Well, we will do self-service maintenance in our range shop, and when we cannot do that anymore, we'll pull them into the impact area and redesignate them as hard targets.

Yessssss . . . finally it was approved, and 40 SUVs with just over 100,000 miles on them became range vehicles, Military police vehicles, logistics vehicles, and more. Everybody who needed wheels loved them."

As a reader you may be saying *"Whoa, didn't you just change the topic on us? Richmond wasn't being given an order that if obeyed would cause harm."*

True. But in a regulation-bound society, we are frequently given compelling or constraining orders about what we must or must not, or can and cannot do, even when our proposal will do good or prevent harm. The true source of the obstacle is essentially invisible. We rarely see the rules that are supposedly written somewhere. We are simply told that the rules prevent doing something. The persons telling us this may or may not have read the rules and considered them in the context of all the other rules and values that apply.

If we give up every time a rule seems to prevent us from doing something creative, positive, and good, we would be displaying learned helplessness, rather than Intelligent Disobedience. Learned helplessness is a phenomenon observed in experiments in which, no matter what the subject tries to do, it cannot meaningfully influence its environment. So it gives up even trying. In a highly regulated society, individuals, and an entire citizenry, can sink into a state of learned helplessness. Cultivating an instinct for questioning rules that seem to defy common sense and developing the art of questioning effectively are core competencies of creative Intelligent Disobedience.

The regulatory society throws up an array of blockages that we need to be willing to test and solve if what we are trying to do is of general benefit. In my work with a wide range of clients, I have found that those who run into a barrier and question it often find the barrier is the result of one interpretation of a situation. Being willing to actively question the ruling finds other interpretations that are just as valid and allows constructive initiatives to proceed.

Too often, the response to regulatory barriers manifests in the form of cynicism or ineffective complaining to others. This is a red flag warning of the condition of learned helplessness. The effective response to walls of regulatory barriers is contained in the observations we made about the successful resisters to the Milgram experiments: asking direct questions that break the mesmerizing spell of authority. Through effective questioning that demands on-point and specific responses, test whether the regulation is legitimate and applicable or if it is incorrectly and counterproductively being applied to the situation at hand. Barry Richmond researched the regulations and asked the right questions.

Richmond encountered a series of such bureaucratic obstacles. As he surmounted each one with resolve and persistence, he developed the self-confidence required to tackle a situation on a scale that may arise only once in a career, similar to Rick Rescorla's ultimate act of Intelligent Disobedience. We can see why Colonel Richmond began his account by asking *What is Intelligent Disobedience?* He astutely asked the question:

> *"Or, even more profoundly, is it disobeying the barriers we ourselves erect to discovering ways to do what is needed in a situation?"*

The Big NO.

The tragedy of 9/11 changed us forever. Now we trained for homeland emergencies with an urgency we had never known, but one we felt day in and day out. We searched for places to conduct realistic emergency response training for our National Guard and state and federal partners. And then, a fellow colonel said, "Barry, I know a place in southern Indiana that would be perfect. It is a state hospital that is closing." I said, "We need something bigger than a hospital." He responded, "Go look at it; you won't believe it." So I went to look at it . . . and I couldn't believe it.

This wasn't a hospital, it was a town! It had a school, a water treatment plant, a sewage plant, a steam generation plant, dining facilities, carpenter shop, electrician shop, a chapel, and on and on . . . fifty-five buildings, most connected with underground tunnels, a 280-acre reservoir, all on a thousand acres. This was Disneyland . . . a training heaven. And the state was going to tear it all down as soon as the hospital closed. We needed this. We had to save it from demolition. But how could we afford it?

Initially, my internal conversation went like this: "Are you out of your mind?!?! How would we ever pay for this!?!? The maintenance cost alone would be over a million dollars annually . . . maybe two . . . or more. No. No. No."

Then Barry Richmond's creative Intelligent Disobedience voice kicked in. Instead of focusing on the barriers and "obeying" them, he looked for the paths around them. After overcoming his internal roadblocks, he was ready to overcome the external roadblocks that were in ample supply. When others in the bureaucracy voiced their own "no," he did not accept this as a signal to "stand down" but looked for ways to bring them aboard. Giving them a taste of the potential in the hospital facility would make the difference in their attitudes.

First things first. We needed to get permission to do a State Homeland Security training exercise while the hospital was still in the process of closing. Most of the buildings had been closed down and were available for the exercise. Yes!

Our soldiers loved it. My bosses, the generals, flew down to check the exercise out. Now they were infected with the "we have got to get this" bug.

One researcher who was studying urban operations training sites came down, and as he surveyed the "city" from a rooftop, he said he had been to all of the urban training centers in the Department of Defense, and this was the biggest and most realistic.

Eventually, the hospital closed. And the state did not tear it down. The governor transferred it to his National Guard and seeded some maintenance funds for transition while we got some federal- and customer-funded support.

A decade has swept furiously by. We have added training venue upon training venue, all designed to offer realism and specialized training scenarios to those who have to operate in complex urban environments. The concept of funding a fully populated "living, breathing city" is still foreign to the military training system. It

breaks all the rules. But the largest Homeland Defense training
event is held there every year, and NATO comes to train. And every-
one who visits says this is the best. And some say, "We want one of
these 'cities' too. How did you ever pull this off?"

We smile . . . and hug our great partners and supporters who
help us wade through the complex swamps that swirl around great
ideas . . . as we scrape off yet another dream-sucking bureaucracy
leech. It's all part of the journey. Endeavor to persevere.

What factors helped Barry Richmond look at each situation and not let a bias for compliance with implicit or explicit rules stop him from looking for that path forward? This is a trained engineer and military man, in other words a man who understands the value of rules and has a sufficient track record of respecting them to be given successively increased responsibilities within the institutions that create those rules.

The reality is that we cannot know all the factors that prepared him to take the creative disobedience stances he took. There were few correlations between life experiences and behavior in the Milgram obedience experiments. What we can know, however, is that Richmond had a deep commitment to the mission for which he was responsible. This is the core requirement of Intelligent Disobedience. Intelligent Disobedience in its full maturity is proactive, not simply reactive to a dangerous order.

Barry Richmond displayed commitment to mission, situational awareness, an autonomous state of mind, a bias for action, and perseverance in the face of barriers. Milgram and our own life experience tell us that we cannot count on the majority of people to naturally display these elements of Intelligent Disobedience. So what do we do?

In all professions and industries where compliance to wrong orders or bureaucratic road blocks can have serious adverse consequences, we need to build the elements of Intelligent Disobedience into both orientation and development programs. The necessity to recognize a situation calling for Intelligent Disobedience can occur on the first day of the job or in the tenth year. Examples of how the culture supports Intelligent Disobedience are needed. Accountability is impressed on all team members. And the culture must be supportive when the team member acts from that sense of accountability.

We have already seen how wide is the range of activities in which Intelligent Disobedience may be needed—from health care, to transportation, to energy, finance, education and the military, to name only a few. All professions have certification programs and continuing education requirements. All companies and institutions have on-boarding processes and professional development opportunities. In addition to teaching the rules, standard procedures, and protocols, they should also design into their curricula modules that teach Intelligent Disobedience and reinforce that training periodically. However well a culture builds the principles of Intelligent Disobedience into the socialization of its young, each profession and each workplace needs to verify that the principles are sufficiently driven home so they are activated when situations call for their unequivocal exercise. We need more Rick Rescorlas and Barry Richmonds. We can wait for them to appear, or we can design our professional development programs and work environments to create them.

Let's review key elements for training a work force in Intelligent Disobedience and supporting its use in the organization culture.

1. Identify likely risks, train people in appropriate responses, practice evaluating situations to determine if those responses should be deployed or if alternative measures—correct violations—should be taken.

2. Train people in the four phases in questions of obedience: cooperation, strain, divergence, and divergence amplification or reduction, and how to consciously use these to do the right thing.

3. Impress on individuals that the earlier they overtly question or object to an inappropriate order, the more likely they will break the mesmerizing effect of authority.

4. Intelligent Disobedience can be done with polite resoluteness, but prepare people to act with determined impoliteness when necessary.

5. Create an organizational norm that, when told policy forbids doing something, individuals insist on seeing the relevant policies to determine if they apply as interpreted to the current situation.

6. Teach creative Intelligent Disobedience using simulations that require networking and agility to imaginatively overcome roadblocks in bureaucratic organizations.

7. Build into orientation and development programs the elements of Intelligent Disobedience as an appropriate balance to the focus on standard operating procedures and policy.

8. As organization leaders, remain supportive when individuals display Intelligent Disobedience in service to the organization's mission and values, even if outcomes are less than desirable.

9. Value and encourage the creative use of Intelligent Disobedience to counteract a culture descending into a learned helplessness that stifles innovation and self-correction.

10. Teach committed perseverance when working to correct unacceptable situations or to find better ways of achieving worthy goals.

Personal Accountability and Cultures that Support Doing Right

I T IS TIME FOR A WRAP-UP OF THE SUBJECT we've been examining. We have looked at the need for Intelligent Disobedience in childhood character development and in professional training. I would like to conclude with reflections on what Intelligent Disobedience can mean at the levels of cultural identity and the evolution of human civilization. Yes, this is a gargantuan step beyond not following an order to cross the street into oncoming traffic. It is my view that the same processes of situational awareness, discernment, and personal accountability operate at all levels of human activity.

The correct role of the individual relative to the group and its authority is as old a question as human society itself. There is always a tension. The tension must be kept in dynamic balance. If the individual is dismissive of authority, a culture cannot maintain its character or operate with sufficient order to protect the rights of other individuals. If authority is dismissive of the individual, it dehumanizes the culture it is charged with serving.

Paradoxically, the culture itself can build into its values and practices the preservation of the individual's freedom against the forces of conformity and obedience it generates. This is the founding American ideal that many other cultures admire and in varying degrees seek for themselves. We are in danger of losing that ideal, and perhaps have already lost it in significant ways.

Our rapidly evolving technology poses a serious challenge. The governing State, and even the commercial "state," can and does acquire practically limitless information on the individuals that comprise it and can monitor every move and activity. If they can be monitored, they can be manipulated or controlled. What are the balances to that power?

Certainly the ability of individuals to use that same technology to inform and organize one another is a counterweight that must be fiercely guarded. An equally fundamental counterweight is the moral development of individuals to resist unwarranted intrusions of authority into our complex social life. Nobel laureate and Polish poet Czeslaw Milosz said,

> *"In a room where people unanimously maintain a conspiracy of silence, one word of truth sounds like a pistol shot."*

True, but we have learned from our reading of Milgram and others that speaking up is just the start. We must develop the capacity to not only speak our truth, regardless of who is wearing the lab coat and holding the clipboard, but to also act on our truth and to support others who speak and act on their truth when authority is misusing power. In other words, we must work as hard at maintaining personal freedom and accountability as we do at creating social cohesion.

As stated at the beginning of this exploration, I view Intelligent Disobedience as a related to, but different than, subject than civil disobedience. Dissent is fundamental to a free society. At times, public dissent leads to civil disobedience as a course for righting wrongs and changing the system. Classic works exist on these topics and should continue to be valued in our culture.

The project in this book is more limited, yet has potentially far-reaching impact: to create a balance to the forces of obedience within existing systems; to create the awareness and norms for resisting unthinking obedience; to instill the values and practice of personal accountability.

These are disciplines that are not a threat to existing structures, but rather a protection against the mistakes or misuses of authority within those structures. They are a protection for both the individual and the true interests of the group. If these habits of character create citizenry more active in questioning the fundamentals of these structures, so be it. It is activism within a system that allows it to transform and adapt in orderly ways and dissipate the pressures that lead to more disruptive reordering.

There have always been individuals who naturally display Intelligent Disobedience. Every great breakthrough in human history has had to challenge or disobey orthodoxy. The greatest examples of these are legendary in our collective minds. Others are less well known but have contributed profoundly to our well-being. A broad range of unjust or unhealthy social conditions have been improved by courageous individuals and groups who have campaigned tirelessly for deep change. Yet, there have also been large numbers of people who have conformed or complied with leaders and movements that have wreaked destruction in their eras.

The intent of Intelligent Disobedience is to prepare greater segments of the population to distinguish between appropriate and inappropriate obedience. It is to develop the cultural expectation and the personal habit of assuming accountability for one's actions, regardless of whether rules or orders come directly from a formal authority figure or indirectly from an unseen bureaucracy or a subculture with distorted values.

There is a fractal structure to nature. Patterns found at the smallest level are successively reproduced at larger and larger levels. An individual who exercises personal accountability and Intelligent Disobedience when warranted on small matters will be prepared to display these skills when large matters are at stake. A society that prepares its youth to be personally accountable and to strike the right balance between appropriate obedience and Intelligent Disobedience will create a vibrant and free citizenry. A culture that exemplifies this balance will serve as a model to other cultures that can find their own expression of these principles.

We can learn some useful lessons from guide dog training, as we should, but the metaphor and techniques cannot be stretched too far. The human psyche, social arrangements, breadth of activities, incentives to instill obedience, and methods of enforcing obedience are far more complex. Even with training in ideal conditions and with dogs bred for the best temperament, not all dogs succeed in mastering the distinction between appropriate and inappropriate obedience. Those that fail are given different roles in life where an error is not likely to prove fatal to the human in its care. Nevertheless, we can use the trusted guide dog as a memorable symbol for the capacity to which we aspire: *to do the right thing when what we are told to do is wrong.*

After fifty years of knowing what Milgram experimentally documented, it is time for our societies to incorporate those lessons, and the lessons learned from related fields, into socializing our young and maturing our professionals. Introducing the skills of Intelligent Disobedience into human development will ensure that in another fifty years we are not still talking with dismay about what Milgram observed; rather, we will be examining how the lessons we applied changed the character of human behavior.

Any human being reading the endless history of inhumane regimes past and present that enslave, imprison, torture, and kill large numbers of their fellow human beings cringes that we have made little, if any, progress in changing this. Unlike Milgram's experiments, these regimes use violence to enforce obedience. How does instruction in Intelligent Disobedience make a difference in that brutal context?

In the short term, the prospects for doing so are limited, but in the long term it can make all the difference. How? We are familiar these days with the concept of the "meme"—a unit of cultural material similar to a gene in biology. If a meme is introduced, finds fertile ground, and is widely reproduced, it eventually becomes part of the societal mindset, of the identity of the group and of the individuals in the group. We are aware of cultures where, for example, honor is central to group identity. An individual in that group would rather risk dying than acquire the social discredit of having acted with a lack of honor.

That is the goal I posit for this work: to instill the values and skills of Intelligent Disobedience at all levels of moral development so that, in future generations, they become an integral part of social identity. Just as you do not want to be considered cowardly, you would not want to be thought of as unthinkingly and irresponsibly obedient.

If that were to occur, then the rise of psychopathic leaders would be nipped in the bud. People around that leader would rather die than bring shame on themselves by blindly obeying a destructive order. They would resist the first instances of such orders before the would-be tyrant could amass power. If the lessons from Milgram's variations on the obedience experiments were inculcated, the first follower who resisted the destructive order would immediately be supported by a second and a third. As Milgram demonstrated, at that point inappropriate obedience drops to its lowest level. There will always be a few who are compliant, but they will be outnumbered, out-voiced, and out-acted by the majority whose identity rests on autonomous responsibility for their actions.

These are lofty, idealistic goals. Nevertheless, they are worthy of being entertained. With the speed of change made possible by social media, perhaps these changes can be manifested within a generation. The question that creates a bridge between today's realities and this potential future though is simple: *What action will you take?*

As a parent, a teacher, an administrator, a manager, an officer, how will you act to create a culture of personal accountability? How will you model that culture? How will you develop group members who view orders and rules as legitimate only when they uphold core values and promote desirable outcomes? Who do right when told to do wrong?

We have heard the stories of what it takes to train guide dogs, flight crews, hospital staff, military personnel, corporate employees, as well as our kids and their teachers in the capacity to comply when compliance is appropriate, to speak up when it is not, and to resist when obeying would do harm. Success is most certain when there has been preparation and practice. The time to develop these competencies is before they are needed. Because they may be needed tomorrow, that time is now. *What action will you take?*

The Courageous Follower: Standing Up To and For Our Leaders

I HAVE MENTIONED TEACHING courageous followership several times in this book. I owe the reader more information on courageous followership for several reasons.

The metaphor of the guide dog that I use is an excellent, but incomplete, model for some applications of Intelligent Disobedience. The guide dog is in no danger of recrimination or retribution for displaying Intelligent Disobedience. In fact, it faces potentially unpleasant consequences only if it obeys a command that it shouldn't.

When you or your employees or your children or students exhibit Intelligent Disobedience, it may not be immediately well received. The authority being questioned has not been trained in responding to Intelligent Disobedience the way the guide dog's handler was prepared for it.

The courageous follower examines ways in which a trusted relationship can be developed with leaders that will support speaking candidly and acting with integrity. It offers many examples of language that could be used in a variety of situations to get the leader's attention, communicate your point with impact, and preserve the relationship. Trying to replicate that material in this book would have weighed it down too much.

Practicing or teaching Intelligent Disobedience does not require the knowledge contained in *The Courageous Follower*. They are very different books, written in service to a common theme of better human relationships, better organizations, and a better world. But the practice of Intelligent Disobedience can be enhanced by a knowledge of courageous followership.

Anyone working in a hierarchy is faced with challenges that occur between those at different levels of the hierarchy. *The Courageous Follower* offers strategies for supporting leaders well and converting hierarchical relationships into productive partnerships.

To further clarify the subject of followership for those who are new to it, the word *follower* is not used as a personality description. *Follower* refers to a role we all play at various times. In medium-sized and large organizations, we often play both a leader role and a follower role.

The book is organized around the principle that followers and leaders both serve the mission of the organization. It examines how they can each do so with strength, offering a model of courageous follower behaviors that has been tested and validated by a generation of researchers interested in followership.

The model consists of five classes of behavior that constitute courageous followership. Briefly, they are:

The courage to assume responsibility—to take action to forward the mission regardless of whether one receives orders or not

The courage to support the leader—to give priority to the leader's direction if it is forwarding the mission and consistent with basic human values

The courage to challenge the leader—to candidly question the leader's assumptions, plans, or behaviors if these are inconsistent with the mission and the values

The courage to participate in transformation—to support the leader's efforts to improve his or her leadership and to work at improving your own performance and behavior in relation to the leader

The courage to take a moral stand—to refuse to participate in an activity viewed as immoral and to take corrective action where possible

Some of the behaviors carry risk, which is why courage is needed. The book examines courage, where it comes from, and how to develop it. This enables courageous follower behaviors to be displayed regardless of whether they are encouraged by the group's leaders.

The book also addresses those in the leader role. It shows why they and the organization are safer if they actively encourage courageous follower behaviors, and it examines how to do so. In that sense, there is a direct relationship with developing Intelligent Disobedience.

In addition to the book, there is a companion Followership Styles Assessment, which can be acquired online. It helps you understand your style of followership, the impact of that style, and how to improve it if desired.

For more information on *The Courageous Follower* please see www.courageousfollower.com or Berrett-Koehler' website at www.bkpub.com.

Notes

Foreword

1. Paul Ricoeur, *The Symbolism of Evil*, trans. Emerson Buchanan (New York: Harper & Row, 1967).

Chapter 2

1. Stefano Passini and Davide Morselli, "Authority Relationships between Obedience and Disobedience," *New Ideas in Psychology* 27 (2009): 98–100.

2. This is a loose summary of the works of developmental psychologists such as Jean Piaget and Lawrence Kohlberg.

3. Passini and Morselli, "Authority Relationships," 100–103.

Chapter 4

1. Robert Baron, "Barriers to Effective Communication: Implications for the Cockpit." www.airlinesafety.com/editorials/BarriersToCommunication.htm

2. David Whyte, *The Heart Aroused: Poetry and the Preservation of the Soul in Corporate America* (New York: Currency Doubleday, 1994).

Chapter 5

1. Valerie Strauss, "Florida Drops Test after Kindergarten Teacher Took Public Stand Against It," *The Washington Post*, September 15, 2014.

Chapter 6

1. Stanley Milgram, *Obedience to Authority: An Experimental View* (New York: Harper & Row, 1974), 17–18.

2. Ibid., 48.

3. Peter Funt, "Smile You're On Candid Scanner," *The Wall Street Journal*, updated November 23, 2010.

4. Milgram, *Obedience to Authority*, 17–18.

5. BBC News, March 18, 2010.

Chapter 7

1. Stanley Milgram, Obedience to Authority: An Experimental View (New York: Harper Perennial Modern Thought edition, 2009) 121.
2. Ibid., 26.
3. Ibid., 77.
4. Ronald E. Riggio, Ira Chaleff, Jean Lipman-Blumen, eds.,*The Art of Followership: How Great Followers Create Great Leaders and Organizations* (San Francisco: Jossey-Bass, 2008); and Barbara Colorosa's work on bullying and genocide.

Chapter 9

1. The data on the "McDonald's compliance event" is taken from a large range of press coverage of the events. The most well-researched coverage was done by Andrew Wolfson in the *Louisville Courier-Journal*, October 9, 2005, in an article titled "A Cruel Hoax: Caller Coaxed McDonald's Managers into Strip-Searching a Worker," which in turn was based on extensive review of original video footage, court transcripts, and interviews of witnesses.
2. Mark van Vugt and Anjana Ahuja, *Naturally Selected: The Evolutionary Science of Leadership* (New York: Harper Business, 2011).
3. Lee Canter, *Lee Canter's Classroom Management for Academic Success* (Bloomington, Ind.: Solution Tree, 2006), 50.
4. Ibid., 51.
5. Ibid., v–ix.

Chapter 10

1. David Nyberg and Paul Farber, "Authority in Education," *Teachers College Record* 88.1 (1986): 4–14
2. Kenneth D. Benne, "The Locus of Educational Authority in Today's World," *Teachers College Record* 88.1 (1986), 15–21.
3. Ibid.
4. John Burnet, ed. and trans., *Aristotle on Education; Being Extracts from the Ethics and Politics,* (Cambridge: Cambridge University Press, 1967).
5. Sharon Presley, "Not Everyone Obeys: Personal Factors Correlated with Resistance to Unjust Authority," Resources for Independent Thinking, Characteristics of Resisters to Unjust Authority, 2010. www.rit.org/authority/resistance.php

6. Nyberg and Farber, "Authority in Education," 4–14.

7. Ibid, 4–14.

8. Cherie Benjoseph and Sally Berenzweig, ModernMom, www. modernmom.com.

9. Leah Davies, "Teaching Children Refusal Skills," www.kellybear.com/TeacherArticles/TeacherTip21.html.

10. Benne, "The Locus of Educational Authority," 15–21.

11. Betsy Eggers, "Intelligent Disobedience," *Atlanta Friends Meeting Newsletter*, October 2010.

12. Lynn Grasberg and Gina Oldenburg, *Great Group Skits: 50 Character Building Scenarios for Teens* (Minneapolis: Search Institute Press, 2009).

Chapter 11

1. James Reason, *The Human Contribution: Unsafe Acts, Accidents and Heroic Recoveries* (Farnham, England: Ashgate, 2008), 223.

2. Ibid.

3. Ibid., 62–65.

4. Andre Modigliani and Francois Rochat, "The Role of Interaction Sequences and the Timing of Resistance in Shaping Obedience and Defiance to Authority," *Journal of Social Issues*, 51.3 (1995), 107–123.

5. Ibid., 73.

Acknowledgments

THE FIRST THANK YOU must go to the participant in my Courageous Follower workshop who brought a future guide dog to class and alerted me to the practice of Intelligent Disobedience. Unfortunately, her name is lost among the hundreds of federal employees who have taken Courageous Follower training.

Next, I must thank my good friend Pat McLagan, and her friends from the Woodside Group, Donna and Larry McNamara, for introducing me to Jim Kutsch, president and CEO at The Seeing Eye, Inc. Jim and Dave Johnson, his director of training, gave generously of their time and knowledge in helping me understand how Intelligent Disobedience training is accomplished with their marvelous dogs, which change people's lives. I also wish to acknowledge Lydia Wade, who for twenty years ran Blue Ridge Assistance Dogs and shared with me her knowledge and love of the service dogs she trained.

Moving on from there, my gratitude goes out to Steve Piersanti, Berrett-Koehler's Publisher, who recognized the value in this project when I first mentioned it to him around 2010. Life sometimes gets in the way of book projects, so Steve hadn't heard more from me about the project for two years. Unprompted, he reached out to express his continued interest. I was appreciative of the constancy of his commitment to the topic and delighted that I could tell him the first draft was nearly ready. Steve then served as my editor on this project, twenty years after serving as editor of *The Courageous Follower*.

My submission of the manuscript then triggered the devoted team at Berrett-Koehler to swing into action. Among them are Jeevan Sivasubramanian, Rick Wilson, Diane Platner, Johanna Vondeling, Kristen Frantz, Mike Crowley, Kat Engh, María Jesús Aguiló, Jonathan Peck, Susan Gall, and their dedicated colleagues.

They in turn harnessed the power of their stable of readers who help BK authors polish their books with skillful feedback from a variety of perspectives. My thanks to Josh O'Conner, Kirsten Sandberg, Maria Lewytzky-Milligan, and Anna Leinberger; Anna did yeoman's service by reviewing the manuscript a second time to help with the final polish.

To this list, I add my own readers, who generously gave me their time and feedback including Rick Shapiro, Sarah Adams Bell, Leith Chaleff-Freudenthaler, and Eli Hager. The book would have suffered from a number of faults these two groups of readers helped me understand and correct. Rick's eagle editing eye, in particular, helped me create a map through the book for readers to follow with trust in where the journey was taking them.

Then there are the 160-plus friends and colleagues and BK champions who provided input into giving the book its name. There was never any question in my mind that *Intelligence Disobedience* would be the title, but they validated that with overwhelming support and helped with the delicate task of finding a subtitle that further conveys the book's topic and rings well to the ear.

Following these good folks are my artistic friends who loaned their practiced eyes to the cover and book design, most especially Debra Witt, founder of Witt's End Design and Branding consultancy in Maryland, and Monica Worth, president of her communications agency, Voice, in rural Virginia.

If this is beginning to read like the credits of a film production, it is because that's what it takes to produce a professionally rendered publication.

The book is replete with stories that make Intelligent Disobedience memorable. The tellers of some of the stories are acknowledged by name, others are lost in the richness of stories I am told orally by folks who approach me during break time or after a presentation: my apologies to the "lost" group. Other friends and colleagues whose valuable stories emerge briefly in the text include Neal Maillet,

Richard Scott Adams, Mary Miller, and, of course, Barry Richmond, whom I quote rather extensively.

Every writer also has a few people close to him or her who provide intimate support. Chief among these is my fellow author and friend Alan Briskin, who gave me counsel at a number of junctions before and during the life of the project, which were invaluable. Thank you, Alan. Don't stop. Similarly, I must thank my fellow author and friend Pat McLagan, who has given me encouragement throughout the process and who has made her home a safe harbor when I am in Washington, DC, and my colleague and friend David Lassiter, who provides another safe harbor in DC, for asking questions that force me to think more deeply about the issues on which I am writing. Added to this group is my former colleague Laurel Davar, who wrote long, thoughtful analyses of how she managed to constructively disobey ill-thought-out orders from a dominating leader of the organization where we toiled together for a number of years.

In the course of my research on Intelligent Disobedience, I became aware of a group of scholars who continue to mine the seminal research of Stanley Milgram. I missed the Obedience to Authority conference they held in Canada in 2014, but one of its co-conveners, Dr. Nestar Russell of Nipissing University in Ontario, referred me to an excellent bibliography on the subject. He also introduced me to another conference on obedience being convened in Kolomna, Russia, by Dr. Alexander Voronov of the State University of Russia for the Humanities in Moscow. I am grateful to "Sasha" for his invitation to present my paper on Intelligent Disobedience to the conference and to several of his colleagues in the field who expressed great interest in the applications of Intelligent Disobedience.

As cited in the book, Marty Krovetz, director of LEAD, an affiliated center of the Coalition of Essential Schools, has been a critical resource for my exploration of obedience in classroom management. Tiffany Sawyer, director of Prevention Services at the Georgia Center for Child Advocacy and Rachel Ballard of Public School Works, pointed me in helpful directions regarding the troubling issues of childhood abuse prevention and the problematic use of seclusion and restraints in schools.

One of my successors at the Followership Community of Learning at the International Leadership Association, Dr. Rob Koonce, did me the great service of introducing me to Dr. Edith Eva Eger, a holocaust survivor and inspirational speaker. Edith, in turn, introduced me to her close associate, Dr. Philip Zimbardo, who graciously consented to writing the foreword to this book at her urging. Their colleague, Steven L. Smith, EdD, also gave much appreciated support for this. Both I and the book are enriched by these connections.

Lastly, I wish to express my appreciation to my partner, Ellen Adams, for her understanding of my need for time to write and rewrite. I am delighted she was able to join me at a Berrett-Koehler author's cooperative retreat and meet some of the many good-hearted and effective souls who share Berrett-Koehler's aspiration of creating a world that works for all.

Index

About the Author

IRA CHALEFF IS THE AUTHOR of *The Courageous Follower: Standing Up To and For Our Leaders*, now in its third edition, and coeditor of *The Art of Followership: How Great Followers Make Great Leaders and Organizations*, part of the Warren Bennis Leadership Series.

Ira has been named one of the "100 best minds on leadership" by *Leadership Excellence* magazine. He is the founder of the International Leadership Association's Followership Learning Community and a member of the ILA board of directors. He was cited in the *Harvard Business Review* as pioneer in the growing field of followership studies. Ira has watched with pride as the concept of followership has moved from obscurity to a topic of study in universities, conferences, and leadership development programs. He is a frequent speaker and workshop presenter on Courageous Followership and transforming hierarchical relationships into powerful partnerships.

Ira is founder and president of Executive Coaching & Consulting Associates, which provides coaching, consulting, and facilitation to companies, associations, and agencies throughout the Washington, DC area. He is chairman emeritus of the nonpartisan Congressional Management Foundation and has provided facilitation to nearly one hundred congressional offices to improve their service to constituents. He is adjunct faculty at Georgetown University, where Courageous Followership is part of the core curriculum in its professional management training for staff. Ira lives in the Blue Ridge Mountains outside of Washington, DC. His daughter, Lily Chaleff, created a beautiful mosaic at the entrance of the property to welcome visitors. Bears frequently disobey the no trespassing signs on the road and help keep his connection strong with the wonders of nature.

Other Books by the Author

The Art of Followership: How Great Followers Create Great Leaders and Organizations, Jossey-Bass, 2006, Ronald Riggio, Ira Chaleff, Jean Lipman Blumen, Editors

The Courageous Follower: Standing Up To and For Our Leaders, 3e, Berrett-Koehler Publishers, 2008

The Limits of Violence: Lessons of a Revolutionary Life, Ira Chaleff as told by Élan LeVieux, Amazon Digital

Berrett–Koehler
Publishers

Berrett-Koehler is an independent publisher dedicated to an ambitious mission: *connecting people and ideas to create a world that works for all*.

We believe that to truly create a better world, action is needed at all levels—individual, organizational, and societal. At the individual level, our publications help people align their lives with their values and with their aspirations for a better world. At the organizational level, our publications promote progressive leadership and management practices, socially responsible approaches to business, and humane and effective organizations. At the societal level, our publications advance social and economic justice, shared prosperity, sustainability, and new solutions to national and global issues.

A major theme of our publications is "Opening Up New Space." Berrett-Koehler titles challenge conventional thinking, introduce new ideas, and foster positive change. Their common quest is changing the underlying beliefs, mindsets, institutions, and structures that keep generating the same cycles of problems, no matter who our leaders are or what improvement programs we adopt.

We strive to practice what we preach—to operate our publishing company in line with the ideas in our books. At the core of our approach is stewardship, which we define as a deep sense of responsibility to administer the company for the benefit of all of our "stakeholder" groups: authors, customers, employees, investors, service providers, and the communities and environment around us.

We are grateful to the thousands of readers, authors, and other friends of the company who consider themselves to be part of the "BK Community." We hope that you, too, will join us in our mission.

A BK Life Book

This book is part of our BK Life series. BK Life books change people's lives. They help individuals improve their lives in ways that are beneficial for the families, organizations, communities, nations, and world in which they live and work. To find out more, visit **www.bk-life.com**.